# Inspired and Outraged

# Inspired and Outraged

The Making of a Feminist Physician

Alice Rothchild

NEW VILLAGE PRESS • NEW YORK

Published in the United States by New Village Press
bookorders@newvillagepress.net
www.newvillagepress.org
New Village Press is a public-benefit, nonprofit publisher
Distributed by NYU Press

Hardcover ISBN 978-1-61332-260-4
eBook Trade ISBN 978-1-61332-261-1
eBook Institutional ISBN 978-1-61332-262-8
Library of Congress Control Number on file.

Cover portrait of the author by Robert Shetterly,
Americans Who Tell the Truth

*Those who do not move, do not notice their chains.*

—ROSA LUXEMBOURG, 1913

*If you have come here to help me, you are wasting your time. But if you have come because your liberation is bound up with mine, then let us work together.*

—ABORIGINAL ACTIVISTS' GROUP, QUEENSLAND, 1970S

*Well behaved women rarely make history*

—LAUREL THATCHER ULRICH, 1976

*I am old enough now to understand that the lessons of history are easily forgotten. This memoir is written for future generations struggling to understand their families of origin, to find their voice and political power, for my daughters Emma and Sasha and nieces Alissa and Daniella, and for their children, Luna, Ori, Cedar and Leland. May they grow and stand tall, grounded in the experiences and wisdom of their foremothers and may their sense of outrage at injustice inform the shape of their lives.*

---

# Contents

## PART THREE: BATTLEFIELD   *109*

In which the battle lines for love and medicine are drawn.

# PART ONE: PRELUDE

In which the yearning for safety and opportunity meets the harsh reality of the depression era and post–World War II USA.

# Genesis

*August 2020*

*Jolly Mountain*

*Okanogan-Wenatchee National Forest*

*Central Washington*

in the rain
straddled across the crotch of
a burned-out hemlock
nuthatches flitting in the branches
my mind turns to memoir.

back to when I was a mere follicle
not even *unborn*
hoping for a sperm destined for greatness.

you will find out later I went to medical school
(before women did *that*)
I'll try to stay away from high falutin' words.
(though spermatogonia is technically more accurate)

this will not be
a hero's journey
(see: sexism)
some triumphal tale leading to a great victory
the slaying of dragons
the meaning of life
the rescuing of damsels.

no, my story is more steppingstones and mud puddles
hands stretched over ravines.

no one dies.
(well, hardly anyone)

by the way, Jolly Mountain?
never made it to the top.

the wind roared like an angry spirit as I remembered
a human pyramid, an act of holding each other up
a woman juggling too many flaming torches.

rain splattered, pockmarking the dry dirt
my hands turned numb in the dense fog
licked by cool clouds puffing up the ridges
like a smokeless forest fire.

# Origins

*1940s*

*Brooklyn, New York*

## Part one

my parents
were wrapped in the sticky fingers
of love
when my mother turned sixteen.

at a party
she spotted
a fine looking guy, eighteen-years-old
thick black curls
a shy smile.

they were neighbors in Brooklyn
children of immigrants
who may have crossed paths at the butcher shop
or the pushcarts in the streets
but never actually met.

she was a good dancer
with beguiling green eyes
the gift of conversation.

he was quiet, smart
an Eagle Scout.

they both learned to swim
in the tidal waves
of the 1929 Great Depression
in Yiddish-speaking families.

## Part two

a couple of decades earlier
their families had huddled
on Ellis Island
surviving two weeks of misery
crossing the Atlantic Ocean
seasick in steerage.

*MANIFEST OF ALIEN PASSENGERS:*

(my maternal great-grandfather)

*Josef Neuberger*
*Nationality: Austria*
*Race of people: Hebrew*
*Last residence: Limburg, Austria*
*Arrival: December 13, 1906*
*Age: 46*
*Gender: male*
*Calling or occupation: painter*
*Able to read/write: yes*
*Marital status: married*
*Final destination: New York*
*By whom was passage paid? son*
*Whether in possession of $50 and if less, how much: $20*
*Whether going to join a relative or friends: 81 Willet Street, NY, son*
*Polygamist, anarchist, mental and physical health, deformed or crippled: no*
*Personal description: 5' 6", fair, blue eyes, light brown hair*
*Ship of travel: Samland*
*Port of departure: Antwerp*
*Manifest Line Number: 0004*

Josef burned the bottoms of his feet
rubbing dirt into open sores
to avoid conscription into Franz Joseph's
Austro-Hungarian army.

he turned his hopes westward
after a long series of business disasters

an empty mill
a cow struck by lightning
a balky half-dead horse
an inn filled with drunken peasants
a flooded lumber yard.

one room with two boarders
the wife and nine children
the sons reaching military age.

a scrappy life surviving on
bread, herring
a wry sense of humor
bolstered by a strong belief in G-d.

hunger and bad luck clung to him
like an ironic punishment from the blessed Almighty.

I heard no other stories
of my peasant folk
the journey from tiny villages
across Europe
likely by wagon and train
boarding a giant steamship
arriving in New York
pinned with manifest tags
identifying information.

(no one spoke English
or knew the English spellings of their names
which morphed with each official transcription
birthdays were best guesses)

I heard no stories
men separated from women
waiting in long lines
for medical and legal inspections
women in babushkas
long skirts
babies swaddled in their arms
bearded husbands and single men
in long peasant coats

lugging bags of feather pillows, comforters
musty from the journey
faces drawn
hearts beating with hope and anxiety.

I heard no stories
of the long metal pens
processing booths
uniformed officials
(inspiring fear, like the tsar's army)
inspecting eyes for trachoma infection
poking stethoscope to chest
listening for the rattle of tuberculosis
letters chalked on clothes.

DENIED
DETAINED
ADMITTED.

as if the stories themselves
weighted with hardship
had dropped into the harbor
like a nightmare
to be forgotten
in *Amerike—der goldene land.*

they all arrived bewildered, penniless
into the raucous tumult of New York City
a son, a father
alone, a young woman joining an uncle
the whole family.

(chain migration)

# Part three

the second of three daughters
my mother was born at home
January 4, 1923
a thorny blossom
in the tangled knot
of her immigrant parents.

every morning her father
washed and shaved meticulously
put on a clean shirt and tie
stood rocking, praying before dawn
wrapped in a tallis and leather phylacteries.

he ate his kosher Farmer's Cheese on dark pumpernickel
drank his coffee with hot milk and tablespoons of sugar
took the subway to the Lower East Side
to sweat long hours in his soaking undershirt
over hot presses in a garment factory.

seventeen dollars a week
no safety regulations
no overtime.

my mother's mother had rolled cigarettes
made artificial flowers for ladies' hats
until Schmuel Lieb Rosner arrived at
Josef Neuberger's doorstep looking for a wife
Josef had many daughters
Berthe was up next
her first love married her older sister
(there was an order to life)
so Schmuel got her.

he liked her ankles
which is probably all he could see
beyond her high cheekbones
steady gaze
long braid twisted around
the back of her head.

my father's father was a shopkeeper
died when his son was five
1925.

cancer.

my father's mother rented apartments
in a brownstone in Brooklyn
yearned to be a real American
lived on the edge of poverty
struggled to love her children
enough.

my parents courted in the shadow of
World War II
worked days
studied nights at Brooklyn College
Rosner sat next to Rothchild.

they both wanted desperately to escape.

1944
just before my father strutted off to war
they were married
in a rushed ceremony
on the only day in the Jewish calendar
weddings are forbidden.

my father wanted to be a fighter pilot
refused -
glasses.

the army sent him to launch weather balloons
in the Philippines.

my mother moved back home
once again sharing a narrow bed
with her sister
worked in a quartz crystal factory
making radios for the war effort.

in 1948
while getting his PhD

on the GI Bill
at the University of Rochester
I was conceived.

his graduation present.

## Secrets

*late 1940s to mid-1950s*

*Brooklyn & Rochester, New York*

*Boston, Norwood, & Sharon, Massachusetts*

my mother tells a story
        part complaint
        part threat
        part lessons learned.

in her crowded tenement apartment
in Williamsburg
the living room chairs covered in plastic
the kosher plates carefully separated
        milk    from    meat
the kitchen perfumed by the aromas of
        chopped liver
                herring
                        brisket
                                pride and poverty
my Yiddish speaking mother
dreamt of becoming
a writer.

in public school
she collected English words
which she found
cold
    unfeeling
        heartless
next to the earthy expressiveness
of Yiddish.

the yearning to write
squirmed inside her
a seed long dormant
a pebble in an oyster.

at night school
she majored in chemistry
never shared her secret
with the handsome guy
she married.

the yearning grew to a loud rumble
words shouting to be heard.

she began to write.
    (in
    secret)

the handsome guy
thought he had a lovely wife
    freshening her hair
        reddening her lips
            putting on a smile
when he got home
to relax in the living room
sip a cocktail
hard day at the office.

the handsome guy
thought he had a good wife
    cooking
        cleaning
            doing laundry
                answering the phone
                    dressing the children
                        putting them to sleep
                            planting forsythia
                                mowing the lawn.

taking care of things.

when he found out
    (the scribbled notes
        a page of manuscript drooped over a manual typewriter
            cigarettes crushed in a ceramic dish)
she says he said

*It's okay for a hobby*
*Just don't take writing too seriously.*

that night he slept on the couch.

in 1951
*Commentary Magazine*
published "The Mothers"
by Sylvia Rothchild.

followed by "The Soldier and His Girl"
        "The Golden Years"
                "A Family of Four"
                        "Thicker Than Water"
                                "End of a Year"
she just couldn't stop.

I thought every mom
had a typing room.

# PART TWO: CHILDHOOD

In which a nugget of ambition clashes with the family's ambivalent assimilation and everyone's expectations for a smart, good girl.

# Modern Childbirth

*November 24, 1948*

*Boston, Massachusetts*

my pregnant mom was due on Christmas.

I was born on the Wednesday
before Thanksgiving
breech.
(butt first)

      SURPRISE!

you could say that
I was always in a hurry
and had a
     lousy
        sense of
           direction.

years later
my mom mentioned
an open labor ward
women screaming
drugged on *twilight sleep*
a concoction of narcotic and amnesiac
that left mothers thrashing
     yelling
        smearing feces
           strapped to their beds with leather belts.

alone.

husbands in the waiting room
paced
   smoked cigarettes
      cigars ready in their pockets.

her contractions were premature
they wouldn't give her
drugs.

she labored
in that big room
echoing with frightened, wailing women
cursing
        crying for their mothers
                tied to their beds
                        harboring babies
                                equally desperate
                                        searching for the way
                                            out.

mother    and    baby
separated
for  the  first  twenty-four  hours  after  birth
to Reduce
        the Risk
                of Infection.

to discourage
        Primitive
                Low class
                        Unhygienic
                                Breastfeeding.

my nose so squashed
docs said
I would need
plastic surgery.

my mother loved me

anyway.

# My Other Brother

*1951*

*Sharon, Massachusetts*

my mother was pregnant
for the third time in three years
it was the 1950s
postwar baby-making.

after my tumultuous arrival
four weeks early
the doc put her on bedrest
for all future pregnancies.

gave her diethylstilbestrol
a fantastical estrogen cure-all
we later found out
caused vaginal cancer in girls
infertility in boys.

she says I took care of her
I was three
my sister
one-and-a-half.

a big job for a small person.

she came home empty-handed.

buried him
in an unmarked grave
nameless.

it was the 1950s.

the night she returned home
my grieving father
went out to play string quartets
while my empty mother's breasts filled with milk
and she held her toddlers close.

she says I took care of her.

clearly not well enough
to save him.

or her.

I always thought she hated Christmas
a tough time for Jews
overrun by Yuletide trees, big-bellied Santas, carols
the orgy of buying and holiday cheer.

now I know
that is when he
died.

taking a spark of her
into that nameless grave.

unspoken grief can be fatal.

the next brother arrived
nine months later
very
premature.

he survived.

miracle boy.

years later I named my dead brother
Samuel
so I could properly say goodbye.

what kind of family
erases its children?

she said Jewish law does not permit grieving a baby
until it has survived for thirty days.

the child was not hers to mourn.

it was the 1950s.

# The Good Times

*mid-1950s*

*Sharon, Massachusetts*

a long wave
of sun-kissed forsythia
shielded us from the street
a hefty pine tree at the end of the lawn
a bank of woods
on the other side.

a weeping willow caressed
the meandering brook
my mother and father dug
draining the land.

homesteading from Brooklyn to
the woods and lakes of Thoreau
church bells built by Paul Revere
baked bean contests on the sweeping lawn
of the Unitarian Church
with pony rides and a jazz band.

I sunbathed naked with my sister and brother
under umbrellas
browning up on our pretend ocean beach
freckled before parents worried about that.

the emerald grass
prickled our toes
the water sprinkler
tossed rainbows in the air
as Mama raked in her garden
moved irises
trimmed roses
dug up skunk cabbage
she had planted in a neat row.
(Brooklyn girl, mistakes were made)

our slinky black cat
white vest like a bow tie
patiently stretched out
in a doll carriage
adorned in a pink baby dress
his ears tweaked by a bonnet
as we played
family.

in 1956 Daddy started a business
New England Nuclear Corporation
making radioactive compounds
for medical research.

(Very Cutting Edge)

we started a business too
The Rothchild Craft Company.

my brother, sister, and I
fingers sticky with glue
mottled with paint
curled over projects
in the chicken-coup-turned-clubhouse
production center
behind the swings and the rows of corn and asparagus.

piles of shells: clam, mussel, cat paw, scallop
Cape Cod bounty
glued into clunky animals
pipe cleaner legs
smiley faces.

we loaded up our red wagon
marched up the hill
to the neighboring development
sold door-to-door
budding capitalists all.

just like Dad.

he took us to his office and lab
on Albany Street in a rundown neighborhood

(yet to be gentrified)
Back Bay, Boston
blew glass straws into curly cues
(milk tasted way better that way)
with a flaming Bunsen burner
filled the air with a smoky chemical fragrance.

I sat at his secretary's desk
licked stamps, folded envelopes
feeling important
useful

grownup.

## Summer Exposure

*1954*

*Sharon, Massachusetts*

silky sand sifted
through my fingers
digging a hole
making fairy castles
leaf flags and pebble walls
at the edge of the sandpit
next to my home
where growling bulldozers
hauled away dirt
to build an exploding exurbia.

a straw-blond kid
a few years older than me
dug his toes into the sand
blue eyes
staring darkly.

he unzipped his pants
yanked out his pale pink penis.

*Wanna ring the bell?*

I stared
frozen
like a fawn smelling
gun smoke.

suddenly
fright shot to flight.

I grabbed my shovel
my pail.

ran across the driveway
up the stairs
to the front door
banging.

fear ate my words
boy-danger-boy-danger-boy-danger.

(never-tell-never-tell-never-tell)

## Humiliation

*1954*

*Cottage Street School*

*Sharon, Massachusetts*

in second grade
I sat next to Barry Buzzewitz
our class like
cupcakes on display
five rows
two-by-two
all vanilla with vanilla frosting.

silent reading
pairs of heads down
palms spread across
open books
mouths moving quietly.

the teacher parked at her desk
exuding the vague grownup smell
of coffee and cigarettes
lost in papers, notebooks
a red pencil tucked behind her ear.

I raised my hand
like the American flag slowly
ascending at assembly
my bladder calling to me
at the wrong time.

there were strict wrong times
in second grade.

impending catastrophe
grew more urgent
my hand shot up like
a jack-in-the-box
my flag waved frantically

whipped by a hurricane of see-me-see-me-see-me
fearful I would pee all over
Barry Buzzewitz's brown canvas neatly tied sneakers.

a warm wetness suddenly spread
between my legs
puddled onto the floor.

*Oh, you poor dear.*

Mrs. O'Donnell hurried over
took my hand
led me to the girls' bathroom
at the back of the classroom.

dwarfing the
child-sized potty and sink
she stuffed scratchy paper towels
against my bottom and crotch.

my classmates whispered and smirked
as I sat down in my damp cotton-only
underpants
a dark stain on my skirt
a soft squishing sound
every time I wiggled.

the price of being
a good, not-too-demanding, speaks-only-when-called-upon

girl.

# Hebrew School

*1955 to 1962*

*Temple Israel*

*Sharon, Massachusetts*

from the time I was seven
Tuesday and Thursday, 3 to 5
Sunday, 10 to 12
Hebrew School.

as we milled about before classes
like corn popping on a hot pan
the principal with the flat red face
blue numbers tattooed on his arm
yelled

> *Sheket B'vakasha!*
> *Line up! Be quiet!*

(one of the few expressions I still remember)

my mother said he was a survivor
wounded by the Nazis
a young man who clung to life
in the death camps
until liberation.

like the rabbi's wife with her tense smile
long delicate fingers
always wore sweaters, buttoned to the top
dressed her children in snow suits in the summer
because she could never get warm enough.

until the day she covered all the furniture in her house
with tinfoil
frightening her two young daughters.

they took her away
psychosis.

my mother said she was a survivor too.

survivor
already I knew
the defining catastrophe for Jews
lucky to be alive
pitied
resilient
forever damaged.

handsome Israeli teachers

(with no teaching experience to speak of)

struggled with unruly, bored children
resentful of More School, Badly Taught
spit balls flew
while we plodded through
>alef
>beit
>gimel
>dalet
>Rosh Hashanah
>Yom Kippur
>Sukkot
>Shemini Atzeret
>Simchat Torah
>Hanukah
>Purim
>Pesach
>Shavuot
>Shabbat.

in Bat Mitzvah class
I learned to keep a kosher home.
>(which my mother had rejected as soon as she could)
I learned the rules for a good Jewish wife.
>(which my mother had greatly amended for herself)
I learned of three thousand years of Jewish history and wandering
>and chosen-ness.

a process of othering
that distanced me from my Cottage Street School classmates

with their Easter Bunnies
and after-school clubs.

I learned to be
a
minority.

# *Bubbe* (Yiddish—Grandmother)

*1950s to mid-1960s*

*Rockaway Parkway*

*Brooklyn, New York*

when we arrived in Brooklyn
the seltzer

(in the refillable blue bottles in the wooden box
at the front of the hall
in the old brick apartment building
with the tiny hexagonal black and white tiles
the entry smelling slightly of urine
on Rockaway Parkway)

after a long squirt of Bosco Chocolate Syrup
sparkled into my milk
and tiptoed up my nose.

a fine reward after hours in the Plymouth
Dad driving from Boston to New York, winding parkways
Mom sitting next to him eyeing the speed limit
watching for bathroom breaks
kids stretched out in the back seat
on the floor, across the back window
reading
            teasing
                    drawing
                            searching for letters on license plates
                                    folding origami cranes.

            *I'm bored. Are we there yet? Stop touching my foot. I said*
                    *stoooop.*
            *Maaaaa. She's touching me.*

my *bubbe* turned the lock, unlatched the door
wrapped each of us into her soft velvety arms
lapsed into Yiddish and a litany of joys and complaints.

we squeezed down the narrow hallway
dragged suitcases to the end
to the kids' bedroom on the right
next to the shadowy shaft filled with stale air
the breath of adjacent apartments
all hugging this vertical lung to the sun.

our goal was to get to the kitchen
       the seltzer
             the chocolate syrup
                the milk.

intoxicated by the sweet and sour fragrance
stuffed cabbage simmering on the stove
chicken boiling in a sea of carrots and onions
chicken fat sizzling with thin slices of caramelized onion
*schmaltz* to *schmear* on the fresh braided *challah*
honey cake begging for our attention.

the floor scrubbed and covered in newspaper
clean for the Sabbath.

the kosher kitchen was as perilous
as it was heavenly
filled with risk, danger
rules to be broken
sensibilities disturbed.

no spoon or plate ever touched the bottom of the sink.
                      a separate drain for milk dishes, meat dishes.
two more sets for Passover.
plus four sets of silverware, milk and meat, regular and Passover.
four sets of pots.

I peered into the fridge cautiously
like crossing state lines into segregated Georgia.

                    *Don't put the milk there, ketzele!*
                      *Don't you see the flanken?*
knishes are they cheese or meat?
                      *Meat near the flanken.*
                    *That's the meat shelf honey.*

gefilte fish can go either way?

> *Near the herring.*

sour cream snuggled next to *lockshen kugel*
okay, that's milk
a jar of *borscht* beamed red purple awaiting the sour cream
everything divided into *fleishig*

> and *milchig.*

even the food had religion.

in the morning I sat on my *bubbe's* white embossed bedspread
fascinated as she wrapped her swollen legs with ace bandages
a ritual I thought universal to *bubbes.*

I waited patiently for her to unwind her frazzled braid.
(promising I would never cut mine)

she brushed out her gold streaked white tresses
      swaying like a blanket of silk threads down to her thighs
           building a gossamer nest in her brush with each stroke
then the slow braiding began
a snake of hair on the side to the middle
      side to middle
         side to middle
tight against her scalp
then swept over her shoulder
wound into a bun tacked up with wide hairpins.

she spent her days cooking, cleaning, walking to the kosher butcher
   the grocer, the fishmonger, seeing relatives, kissing children
      waiting for our Friday night phone call
         sitting by the window watching the traffic on the stoop
           the people with their shopping carts and baby carriages
              a lone catalpa tree marking the seasons.
her own little *shtetl.*

she never learned to read or write and wasn't quite sure about TV.

she waved at the super
who lived in the apartment next door
he took care of the place
checked the coal bin

swept the entry
she called him the *schvartze*
what did she know from Black People?

like a sentry
hours sitting at her bedroom window
was she dreaming of the old country?
the pond
chickens
forest dense with trees
her vibrant father with his thick red beard
      charismatic seders
            deep singing voice?

did she have regrets?

I was told when she got married she was expected
to cut her hair short
wear a wig (a *sheitel*)
like a good Jewish wife.

she refused.

it was her only act of
      rebellion.

# Teeth in a Jar

*1950s to mid-1960s*

*Rockaway Parkway*

*Brooklyn, New York*

at night
my *bubbe*'s teeth
slept in a jar
in a clear medicinal smelling liquid.

two rows of white chompers
attached to a horseshoe
of pretend pink gums
sat in a glass on her night table
a freaky fascinating discovery
for a child.

in the dusky light I peeked at
her fallen-down face
looking like a vaguely familiar
puppet
with a muffled mouth.

was that really her?
would she be embarrassed
if I stared?

could I still kiss her?

those silent teeth
what stories would they tell?

moments of tenderness
homespun Yiddish-inflected wisdom
secrets held in tight clench
swept by an old tongue
grabbing sorrows
before they could
escape.

her home-grown teeth
had they rotted
fallen out when
she was young
grabbed by a dentist
who had nothing else to offer
a poor immigrant lady?

did she save for months
to pay for their replacements?

what happened to the
precious false teeth
when she died?

were they tossed in the garbage
as if her words
and self-respect
never really mattered?

at night
my *bubbe*'s teeth
slept in a jar

waiting to be useful.

# Aunt Sadie

*1950s to 1960s*

*Sharon, Massachusetts & Brooklyn, New York*

the acrimonious rage pounded against
Aunt Sadie's subdued sobbing
her face shielded in her hands
Uncle Max sitting upright in the rocking chair
on the covered porch
at our house.

I hid in the hall, the smell of tobacco and hurt
drifting my way
listening like a tiny big-eared bat
picking up sonar signals
danger ahead.

I had no words for verbal abuse
posttraumatic stress disorder
but knew something was terribly wrong.

I knew
(the way a child intuits from the air
the glances
the unsaid
the hushed voices)
Uncle Max returned from his stint
in World War II
a three pack-a-day smoker with a wide smile
and a short temper.

what was he like before?

the black and white photos show them
smiling, hand-in-hand
in love.

he stayed around long enough
to produce a son
and get shipped off to fight.

what horrors had he endured?

he survived the war but
not the cigarettes.

LUNG CANCER.

the day they got the phone call
my mother and father stopped smoking.

ashtrays collected buttons and dust.

I watched as my
my mother's older sister
grieved her fantasy of a perfect husband
for the rest of my childhood.

she raised her only son
worked as a medical secretary
took her ghost of an elderly father
into her home
a small Brooklyn apartment lined with old photos
of her Bar Mitzvah boy
and her dead husband in full military gear
grinning.

she was my favorite aunt
            patient
                        long-suffering
                            loyal
                                    giving
                                        giving
                                            giving.

I always wanted to be
good

like her.    .

# Incorrectly

*1953 to 1960*

*Cottage Street School & Sharon Junior High School*

*Sharon, Massachusetts*

every day, elementary school started
with a scraping of chairs
bodies straight
eyes staring at the red, white, and blue
drooping next to the blackboard
a fake gold eagle perched at the top of the pole
hands on our hearts.

(which got increasingly difficult
when breasts started to erupt)

Where exactly do I put my hand?

> *I pledge allegiance to the flag*
> *of the United*
> *States of America . . .*
> *under God. . . .*

followed by the Lord's Prayer

> *Our Father who art in heaven*
> *hallowed be thy name.*
> *Thy kingdom come.*
> *Thy will be done*
> *on earth as it is in heaven . . .*
>
> *Amen.*

by the end of fifth grade
I mouthed the words silently
too Christian for me
afraid to stand out
or cause a fuss
and I wasn't that sure about God.

[June 25, 1962
US Supreme Court declared
prayer in public schools
unconstitutional]

we were graded on
        Sits
                Stands
                        Walks Correctly
Satisfactory
        Needs Improvement
                Unsatisfactory.

as if the ability to
        sit quietly at a desk
        stand up without slumping or hitting the kid in front of you
        walk in a straight line

predicted some kind of future success
or special intelligence.

rather than the ability
to be a quiet functional cog
in some very big grinding patriarchal capitalistic God machine.

which maybe was the goal
of elementary education.

by junior high
at the end of each day
the principal's voice droned over the loudspeaker
announcing The Detention List.

the same bad kids over and over.

now I know this was probably the list of misfits
with ADD
        ADHD
                dyslexia
                        autism
                                depression
                                    anxiety
                                        family trouble

poverty
boredom

each with their own special gifts, weaknesses, needs, and styles of
learning.

all unmet.

Amen.

## Almost

*November 1958*

*Sharon, Massachusetts*

for days
(perhaps weeks)
as the air chilled
the grass browned
froze like stubble
on a wrinkled cheek
my mother crept into bed
and did not get up.

I watched
hacking cough
flushed face
a snow bank of crumpled tissues
by her bed.

the languid medicinal fragrance of lotion
(did I rub it on her aching back?)
feverish sweat
rumpled hair
no lipstick.

at Massachusetts General Hospital
the doctors said her chest x-ray
was *whited out*
another snow storm.

she missed my birthday.

children were not allowed in patients' rooms
a kindly lady with a pale face and crimped hair
took us to the dim chapel with the arched doorway.

> *Pray for your mother.*

I held my sister and brother's hands tight and told her

*We're Jewish.*
*We can't pray here.*

mommy almost didn't come home.

double pneumonia
lungs filled with bacteria and pus
crowding out the steady inhalation of breath.

when she limped back to her bed
she sewed me a stuffed blue corduroy horse's head
to hold in times
of emergency.

# Sixth Grade Christmas

*December 1959*

*Cottage Street School*

*Sharon, Massachusetts*

we were the gifted class
seventeen girls
five boys
mostly Jewish.

we finished the year's curriculum
pretty much by December
spent much of the month
building Santa's paper train filled with boxy presents
chugging across the windows of the one story brick building
decorating the Christmas trees
(that graced every classroom)
with paper chains, snowflakes, glittery pretend icicles.

every morning we caroled
from class-to-class.

*Silent Night, Holy Night*
        jammed in my throat
        knifing my dawning sense of otherness.

Jeffrey Ruben and I
won the Christmas mural contest
devoted hours to cutting and gluing
tissue paper angels and gossamer wings
        a fantasy I could not embrace
a faux stained-glass window for the front display
across from the principal's office.

turning the school into
a church.

Jewish parents complained
a town meeting turned ugly.

under the glare of reporters
townsfolk marched
waving placards and chanting

> *The Jews are destroying Christmas!*

it made the national news.

inside my quiet weeping place
I knew

> I am less than welcome
> a minority
> a Jew
> in a Christian country
> fourteen years after the end
> of the Nazi Holocaust.

> more angry
> hurt
> frightened

> than jealous.

# Ballet School

*1959*

*Sharon, Massachusetts*

in sixth grade I loved
Rima my diminutive ballet teacher.

> with her sinewy legs
> flat muscular stomach
> curved arches
> pointed toes
> perfect Boston Ballet turnout
> tight bun
> every hair in place
> exuberantly painted eyelashes.

by then I was taller than her
hips roomier
shoulders wider
breasts more
> Marilyn Monroe than
> waif-like Audrey Hepburn.

> (every other girl in class
> *jetéing* about in a training bra)

> > I hated
> > my curvy
> > soft
> > womanly
> > body.

> > hated it.

> > so

> > much.

# Talent Show

*1960*

*United Synagogue Youth, Temple Israel*

*Sharon, Massachusetts*

there was an undaunted daring
in me
in my dark leotard
wrapped in silky pink, yellow scarves
and graceful aspiration.

the basement lights bright
gleaming the black linoleum floor.

my mother in the wings
the record player's scratchy entrance
as needle hit vinyl.

I danced, swirled
a pirouette, a jeté, an arabesque
was it Tchaikovsky? Ravel?
Israeli folk music?

the youth group
twenty or so brooding teenagers
cupped along the paneled walls
did not appreciate my artistic efforts.

my audacity suddenly
        crushed
            ·      shamed
                    by the growling chant
                        of jeering teenage boys.

*She's gonna strip.*
        *She's gonna strip.*
                *She's gonna strip*
                        ·   *strip*
                            *strip.*

## Menstruation

*1960*

*Sharon, Massachusetts*

I awoke to an odd sensation
my sheets and nightgown stained a rusty brown
my thighs wet, plum red
a vague ache in my belly.

I marched proudly into my parents' bedroom
(off limits to children)
and announced:

> *Today I am a woman!*

at school, my secret sang in my ear
I had crossed the threshold
plunged down the rabbit hole.

on my calendar I drew a tiny *p*
every 28 days for months ahead
innocently unaware that
the female body is not a machine
that adolescent ovaries
are as unpredictable
as
adolescents.

several moons later
I squatted half-naked in the bathtub
the pink shower curtain pulled tight
clutching a tampon
smeared with Vasoline
my mother sitting on the closed toilet seat
offering directions
inviting me into the sisterhood
of women
who walk around without saggy smelly pads between their legs
hitched up with belts and tabs.

who go to the beach, wear a bathing suit.

who don't worry if it is that *time of the month*
when we have our periods
which we ironically call
*our friends.*

a joke was whispered between Audubon camp counselors the
     following summer
(I was a counselor since I looked older than I was since I was, after
     all, a woman)

> *How do you punctuate fun fun fun worry worry worry?*
>
> *Fun period*
> *Fun period*
> *Fun no period*
> *Worry, worry, worry.*

I didn't get it.
I was only twelve.

but I laughed loudly
anyway.

# The Wreck of The Hesperus and Other Things

*1959*

*Sharon Junior High School*

*Sharon, Massachusetts*

7-1-A (later called the gifted class)
saved my life and wrecked
countless others.

> 1-A to be distinguished from 1-B, 1-C (all smarties)
> 7-2A, 2-B, 2-C, (average- but not definitely college
>     bound)
> 7-3-A, 3-B, 3-C (aka the dumb kids)
> (see: needs unmet)

the aging Mrs. Langley chortled
we were
all too smart to study grammar
> hence my lifelong struggle with the
>     pluperfect
not to mention a certain haziness about the use and abuse of the
    semicolon;

we were assigned to find a poem
and memorize it
I wanted something long, hard, and spectacular.

I chose *The Wreck of the Hesperus* by Henry Wadsworth Longfellow.

every night I repeated eight new lines
until all 88
rattled easily in my head
and off my tongue.

the teacher was so smitten with my performance
she made everyone learn

> *It was the schooner Hesperus,*
> *That sailed the wintry sea;* (behold the semicolon!!!)
> *And the skipper had taken his little daughter,*
> *To bear him company.*

made the entire class recite the whole damn poem at assembly.

when the dreaded line

> *The salt sea was frozen on her breast*

came looming
the class went silent
no one willing to say
the embarrassing, sexually suggestive word

> *breast.*

but my eager voice rang
unmistakable, unencumbered.

> *BREAST*

reverberated over my muted classmates
washed across the entire seventh and eighth grade
squirming in the dark auditorium.

perhaps I should have kept my mouth shut.

being a smart, driven, outspoken girl
left its own kind of
wreckage
on the barren shores
of my hard-to-endure
teenage loneliness.

## Home Economics

*1960*

*Sharon Junior High School*

*Sharon, Massachusetts*

in shop
pubescent boys
hammered bookshelves
gun racks.

whacked thumbs
sanded off fingertips
lugged wood.

manly stuff.

girls practiced their
homemaker skills
the opening dance to
wifedom and motherhood.

we decoded recipes
cracked eggs
debated tablespoon over teaspoon
baked cookies and lemon squares
the perfume of vanilla and sugar
wafting through our
edible science lab.

we spread crackly dress patterns
across desks
sandy brown paper etched
with blue lines, arrows
tightly printed
step-by-step directions.

FRONT
BACK
COLLAR
SLEEVE

found selvage edges
grain of weave
pinned cloth to paper
snipped scissors to cloth.

I cut out pieces
to a dreamy lavender dress
fingers dusted with tailor's chalk
pinned darts and seams
basted loopy stitches
joined the other girls in the
clickity-clack whir and chatter
of sewing machines.

at the end of the year
the school held a
fashion show.

girly stuff.

by then
I had grown so much
the dream dress was
a high-waisted monstrosity
squashing my boobs
exposing my knobby knees
as I awkwardly twirled
and sashayed
across the assembly stage.

teeth clenched
smile frozen
performing.

possibly
good practice for 1960s
wifedom and motherhood.

plus, I could feed myself
bake a cake
fix the occasional loose button

mend a torn knee patch
thread a bobbin.

cooking and sewing.

the most enduring lessons
from the wasteland that was
junior high school.

# For You

*October 12, 1960*

*Cape Cod, Massachusetts*

Daddy! Daddy! Daddy!
See Me! See Me!
Love Me! Love Me!

(I was twelve and that mattered)

Columbus Day, dunes sparkled as seagulls squealed
diving at tattered fish carcasses
eviscerated horseshoe crabs
cloaked in seaweed
exuding a salty rot.

you dared me to swim in the icy grey waters with you.

I didn't want to freeze or
ruin my carefully straightened hair.

(I was twelve and that mattered)

I plunged in like an Arctic mermaid.

when we dashed out
stumbling over rocks
like piles of briny marbles
waves thumping our goose-bumped legs
shivering
blue-toed
you teased me
for my frizzy
salty
messy
curls.

I wrapped my chilly shoulders
in a thin blue beach towel
teeth chattering
covering my body, shamed and hiding.

(I was twelve and that mattered)

Daddy! Daddy! Daddy!
See ME!
Love ME!

# Bananas

*Late 1950s to mid-1960s*

*History class, Sharon, Massachusetts*

we folded paper turkey tails
crayoned stuffy men in black hats
        square collars
                large buckled shoes
bronze skinned Indians in splashy
        feathered headdresses.

high on the addictive drug of
America the Beautiful
dosed with progress, morality
superior (European) civilization
everything's always gonna be okay
        for us.

decent, sturdy Pilgrims
arrived on a rickety boat
feverish, seasick, unwashed
three months of
        hardtack
                biscuits
                        dried meat
                                beer.

harboring
        Bibles
                guns
                        smallpox
                                yellow fever.

hoping to celebrate their kind of religion
a chance for land
a belly full of food.

we saw nice white people
planting corn with the Wampanoag Indians

munching turkey (didn't ever doubt they had stuffing
cranberries
pumpkin pie)

learning how to sow and survive
tap maple trees
catch river fish
avoid poisonous plants.

learning from generous, naked *savages*
who shared their wisdom
peaceably
saved the settlers' lily white butts
from a frigid New England winter.

we learned nothing of
Indian laws and customs
egalitarian societies
matriarchies
respect for earth, sun, and sky
the beauty and power of song
poetry
history told father to child.

we learned nothing of
deceptions, massacres
atrocities in the service of progress
and Christianity
weaving a giant web of nationhood
in the spirit of
Columbus in the Americas
Cortes in Mexico
Pizarro in Peru
the genocidal frenzy for gold and slaves.

how many white men
discovered lands
already taken?
honored?
loved?

in 1959 when Batista was overthrown by Castro
       US corporations and wealthy businessmen
       owned half of Cuba's sugar plantations
       most of its cattle ranches, mines, utilities.

communism looked like a definite improvement
but no one talked about *that*
it was the cold war
the enemy lapped at our shores.

I knew about JFK's 1961 Bay of Pigs fiasco
it was in the newspapers
      on the radio
      dinner time chatter
rag-tag CIA-directed anti-Castro Cubans
bungled an effort to invade the island
ships sank in coral reefs
paratroopers landed on the wrong beach
they surrendered in twenty-four hours
one hundred fourteen dead
over a thousand taken prisoner.

hard to miss
even at twelve.

my history classes skipped a host of American calamities
we read *Uncle Tom's Cabin, Gone with the Wind*
the poetry of Langston Hughes
tiptoed around *difficult* issues
that didn't fit the American myth-making machine.

in my early teens
I wishfully entered a poetry contest for
the next ad for Chiquita banana
(formerly United Fruit Company).

       I knew nothing of the
       exploitative plantations
       United Fruit
largest employer in Central America 1930s
single largest land owner in Guatemala

            triggered Costa Rican banana strike 1934
                  CIA coup in Guatemala 1954
                     to install a pro-business
                        military dictator.

ever hear of a *banana republic*?

none of this was in my true-blue
all American
wave-the-flag
eagles-soaring-in-the-sky
neatly-sliced-bananas-on-cornflakes
curriculum.

# Summer Camp

*1961*

*Red Fox Music Camp*

*Great Barrington, Massachusetts*

practice sheds
dotted the old farm
scales and arpeggios
sent as daily offerings
to the gods of
Bach, Mozart, Beethoven
piano sonatas erupted like dandelions
flutes competed with bird song.

violin in the morning
piano in the afternoon
a good book in between
heaven.

perhaps I was deranged
by the ambrosia of sweet grasses
the night sky salted
with the Milky Way's billion intergalactic sparks
the random comet
streaking across the heavenly sky
heightened by teenage hormones
devoid of parental regulation.

I fell hard for a Hungarian violinist
his pathos, his musical genius, his thick sandy curls
he fled Budapest and the Hungarian Revolution
as a child
his mom refused to leave
he walked across Europe
at night
with his dad.

he arrived in New York
a hungry frightened child prodigy.

his story made me weep.

we spent the summer debating
the pro and cons of
holding hands
intimacy was not his strong suit.

I fell (more cautiously)
for a tall, talented trumpet player
with straight blond hair
great lips
eager and determined
the first time we leaned in
for a kiss
our glasses got so tangled up
our lips never
actually touched.
(I wanted to die)

on Wednesdays, the cook had her night off
the lively Italian camp director
left the ivory keys of her grand piano
sweating the afternoon away
over large vats of tomato sauce
pots of spaghetti
bread
thickly layered with garlic.

in the evening
the camp held a weekly *social*
with the kind of music
normal kids listened to.

I always wondered if the garlic bread
was an anti-kissing device
an early attempt
at birth control
in the rollicking Berkshire Mountains.

# 800

*1962*

*Sharon, Massachusetts*

800
calories
a
day.

one
solitary
egg 72
half a grapefruit 41
three-and-a-half ounces
skinless boneless chicken breast 163
my constant companions
my cheerleaders
my guides.

lists of every bite
measured and counted
every trip to the scale
damning and recorded.

my body
reflected in a funhouse mirror
bulged and contracted
as I stared at my (distorted) image
a judgment every morning
a list of flaws
areas for improvement
that sense of absolute control
mastery
my soft hips
full breasts
melting away
turning
my

clock
backwards.

puberty, not really welcomed in my family
(I knew at some primal level)
my Mother Felt Threatened
another (sexual) woman in her house
my Father Felt Confused and possibly Aroused
another (sexual) woman in his house.

I wanted desperately to be less
to be twiggy thin and androgynous
child body/cool teenager
skinny was in.

I wanted in.

twenty-five pounds and months of no period later
my father dragged me to Massachusetts General Hospital
Dr. Janet Ward McArthur
first female professor Harvard Medical School
a big bosomed general
on a battleship of disapproval.

she told my father
I had to regain all that meticulously lost weight.

*No Ifs Ands Or Buts.*

he took me to Durgin Park
with its long wooden tables
monster slabs of roast beef
waitresses that yelled across the room
called me
*Hon.*

*Eat* he said.

still an obedient child
I did.

twenty-five pounds later
my underwear soaked
in unexpected menstrual blood

I grieved my destiny:
fat unattractive unfashionable.

Possibly
Unlovable.

never really made peace
with food
with loving the hungry
sensual
healthy
female body
that was mine.

never really figured out
how to feed

myself.

## View from Abroad

*August 26, 1963 to September 22, 1963*

*Israel, Italy, Switzerland, Denmark*

I first understood
that my family
was embraced by the golden hand
of opportunity and prosperity
when my dad announced
he was taking us all to Israel and Europe
for three weeks.

A Very Big Deal.

my first gigantic family adventure
flying ten hours over an ocean, six miles high
to the place we called
our homeland
all magic, hot, hopeful
like me.

I kept a snarky, awestruck diary
filled with details of each day.

like a detective on assignment
I (obsessively) catalogued
every saber cactus in the promised land
croissant in France
death-defying taxi ride in Italy
every train, hotel, time of arrival, departure
the detritus of tickets, postcards, announcements, candy wrappers
details stuck between pages like pressed flowers.

an endless stream of adolescent social commentary
curiosity and disdain about foreign tongues, foreign people
amused by the mishaps of travel.

my sister bumped the table
spilled my brother's hot chocolate in his lap

in a café overlooking Lake Lugano
why did I want to remember that?

my dad had meetings
at the Weitzman Institute and Technion in Israel.

(we saw the Dimona nuclear reactor which officially did not exist)

my mom (with her press card)
interviewed Holocaust survivors
Russian and Moroccan Jewish immigrants, Israeli youth
while my sister, brother, and I
frolicked in one pool after another
in the unrelenting Mediterranean sun
and I flirted with a Moroccan waiter
named Hananya
at a hotel in Herzliya.
(to my father's astonishment)

momentous explores with my family in
Rome
Lugano
Copenhagen
Paris.

out of Israel, I waxed eloquently about
the upgrade in plumbing
my first bidet
impressed by grand European hotels
ancient fountains, epic squares and churches
superhuman-sized statues in the Vatican museum
titillated by the attention from men staring at my sister and me.
(not happy with the pinches on crowded buses in Rome)

on a street with my father
a man thought I was his girlfriend
started serenading.
(me—pleased—
shocked)

first class sleeper train
from Switzerland to Denmark

my mother anxious, still unwilling to set foot
in post-war (Nazi) Germany
the cities
flashed by as the train rocked
through the night
names I only knew from the war.
(trains still an echo
of cattle cars and death camps)

Paris on Rosh Hashanah
crowded into the women's section
of the Baron Rothschild's temple
(not my namesake)
looking down from the balcony
on men in black silk hats
like giant chess pieces
organ music discordantly saturating the cavernous hall
(is that really Jewish?)
I cried through the service
wrote dramatically
*It's hard to be a Jew in Paris.*

I saw Europe through my mother's eyes
glorious architecture
quaint villages
spectacular food
tainted by the Gestapo and Vichy France.

September 15
first day in Copenhagen
a pre-dinner date with a Supreme Court judge.

I was vaguely aware of the screaming headlines:
WHITE SUPREMACIST BOMBING
16th Street Baptist Church
Birmingham, Alabama
Ku Klux Klan
nineteen sticks of dynamite
four black girls murdered.
(three my age)

The Danish judge smiled
offered us a plate
of exquisite pastries
tea
turned toward my mother.

*Is Birmingham a typical American city?*
he asked.

as my mother arranged her face
he shook his head.

*How can you raise your children*
*in such a dangerous country?*

# Growing Up and Liking It

*Late 1950s to mid-1960s*

*Sharon & Brookline, Massachusetts*

when I was a teenager
my mother left discreet
brochures on my pillow
with names like

> *Growing up and liking it*
> *Getting to know your body*
> *Your period and you*

with pictures of white boys and girls
in baseball caps, poodle skirts and bouncy pony tails
smiling
holding hands
licking ice cream cones.

I stared at the anatomical drawings
but never tried any in-person verification.

there were clear warnings about
the importance of

## HYGIENE

bathing
douching (yes douching—the vagina being one of those dirty little
      places
that needed a certain amount of upkeep)
deodorant.
(my obviously gay but I-never-figured-that-out-in-high-school gym
      teachers
were extremely serious about
hygiene)

in this very hetero very white very middle class
brochure
there was one other message

Girls: Save Your Virginity for the Big Night!!!

> warning: no boy is gonna respect a girl
> who is too *easy*
> one girl, sophomore year
> got herself pregnant
> married her
> high school sweetheart
> but that didn't seem right either.
>
> WARNING!
> WARNING!

this was an improvement over
my mother's experience
when she came to her own mother
bleeding, weeping
afraid she had some fatal disease
her gentle, loving never-hit-a-fly of a mother
slapped her across the face
an old Eastern European Jewish custom
designed to keep menstruating girls
out of trouble
and trouble out of menstruating girls.

my mother spent a lot of time
in the biology section
of the local Brooklyn library.

at this point I had a pretty decent idea
about Anatomy
a vague understanding that
millions and billions of sperm came blasting out of a penis
after the guy had wiggled around down there
in some special juices.

(maybe like slug slime??? definitely unclear—
along with the concept of The Erection)

then (was I envisioning thousands of salmon swimming upstream
or herds of horny buffalo galloping across the plains?)
those little tadpoles dashed

valiantly north on a river of exceptional goo
until they found the lovely
eyelash flapping, passive little egg
all primped and ready

Winner Take All!

BINGO!

bingo was to be avoided
until there was a ring on your finger
and you were mature enough
to raise a family.

it wasn't until college
that I finally figured out that
his thing actually goes INSIDE my thing
a detail those brochures (and my mother) failed to mention.

along with how that moment actually felt
the slow dance
the heart pounding anticipation
the melting of flesh
all velvet, peaches, and cream.

I grew up and
liked it.

# Nuclear Daffodils
## (version published May 2021 Ariel Chart)

*1960s*

*Sharon, Massachusetts*

in my town
people, like gophers
tunneled into their front lawns
building bomb shelters
the telltale air vents
sticking out of the grass amidst the daffodils.

they hoarded box-loads of canned food, dry goods
for the long nuclear winter
what would be left when they came up for air?
glow-in-the-dark water?

in my town
duck and cover drills in junior high school
that cavernous old building with tall windows
and uneven floors
echoing with pimply, unruly teenagers
sweaty hormones
Elvis Presley's
blue suede shoes.

me with my hair teased like cotton candy
lips glowing burnt orange
my aching loneliness
a constant companion.

I never understood how hiding under the desk
as it slid on the buckled school floor
and those old creaky windows
exploded from the bomb blast
would protect me
from nuclear
oblivion.

on sweater day
boys loaned bulky jerseys and pullovers
to their sweethearts
girls flaunted their trophies
in the halls between classes
during recess.

my very gay history teacher lent the girls
without boyfriends cardigans perfumed
with his sweet, manly smell.

I felt held, comforted, special
freed from sweater-less shame.

but there were bigger things
to stress about.

nuclear armed missiles on Cuba
right off our southern coast.

photos
of the mushroom clouds over Hiroshima and Nagasaki
shimmered in my anxiety.

in my town.

# Forbidden Fruit

*late 1950s to mid-1960s*

*Sharon & Brookline, Massachusetts*

my daddy
did not want
*You ain't nothing but a hound dog*
gyrating in his house.

my sister, brother, and I listened
crouched defiantly around the record player
gorging on forbidden fruits
when he was out.

my very liberal, educated, cultured mom
thought Bob Dylan
was Black.
*The times they are a changin'*
blowing into her protected air space.

       "Ma. He's a Jewish kid from Minnesota.
       Bobby Zimmerman."

(grandson of Ukrainians and Lithuanians
for god's sake)

so I guess it's not a surprise, in high school
I played a Beethoven sonata
for the school talent show
black cocktail dress
pearls
wobbly high heels
months of diligent practice
on those silver tongued ebony and ivory keys.

I glanced at the hundreds of faces
fading into the dim balcony
theater lights scorching my eyes.

the hissing and booing started slowly
growing to a low thunder

growling at the dance of notes and chords
emanating from my fingers.

teeth clenched, shoulders tight
doggedly resolute
the bellow of teenage shaming
screaming in my ears.

> *Don't listen to them, honey.*
> *What do they know?*

(I do love Beethoven)

senior year
I teamed up with three women
similarly inclined
started a secret girl-band
*The Group*
hemmed our skirts mid-thigh
parted our hair in the middle
long beads
channeling Joan Baez
I played electric piano
belted out songs like a rock star.

TALENT SHOW.

I could feel the collective dread
radiating from our classmates
as they stared at our choir robes
we launched into a madrigal
all serious and medieval.

suddenly the curtain swooped up
        exposing a drum set!
                electric guitars!
                    piano!

we dropped our robes.

the drummer jumped onto her stool
thumping, pulsing,
head bobbing

the first chord
a clarion call.

*HANG ON SNOOPY, SNOOPY HANG ON.*

my classmates screamed!
       shouted!
              surprised!
                  delighted!
                        relieved!

sweet revenge.

cool kid for a day.

# Female Initiation Rites

*Mid-1960s*

*Sharon & Brookline, Massachusetts*

BP—before pantyhose—
I dutifully wriggled
into a tight white
girdle
the crisscrossing bands of elastic
literally crushing my internal organs
sending my guts north
where my lungs
were supposed to be
flattening my rounded belly
curvy hips
into some idealized
version
of
woman.

boyfriends found that wall of elastic
a definite challenge
in the frantic efforts
to get to the next
base
my body being
an athletic
playing field.

I felt safer that way.

my mother wore a
Black Merry Widow
the 1960s version
of a whale-bone corset
garter straps
to hold up her nylons
with the seams in back

and push up her
boobs.

I never figured out
exactly how she peed
in that contraption.

I did learn that to be
attractive
as a woman
I had to
correct my flaws.

BANGS
>> to hide my
>> not-big-enough forehead.

EYEBROWS TWEEZED
>> to give the optical
>> illusion that my eyes
>> were not
>> too close together.

VERTICAL STRIPES
>> to camouflage the
>> exact dimensions of my
>> butt.

shaved my legs and armpits smooth
blushed my cheeks peachy pink
swabbed a hint of blue eye shadow
slept on three inch rollers
to straighten my
thick kinky hair.

wore clunky high heels.

>> (not good for running)

hemmed my skirts mid-thigh.

>> (not good for sitting)

skipped breakfast, avoided butter, ice cream, fried foods, bread,
   cheese.

> (not good for
> having all the energy
> and feistiness
> necessary
> to march through
> another contested day)

I was quite
an improvement project.

# A Pearl of a Girl

*November 1964*

*Boston, Massachusetts*

sweet sixteen
kissed kissed kissed
never got beyond
that base.

remember bases?

(thank god for summer camp)

not enough friends
for a
party party party
no boys anyway
dared to *like* me
smarty pants, straight A's
goody goody two-shoes.

symphony hall
Daddy, Daddy, Daddy,
took me to a concert
on a Saturday night.

pearls and heels
peach blush on my cheeks.

(thank god for Beethoven
inscribed above the stage)

sweet sixteen
better, better, better
than moping at home
feeling special, special, special
in that great big hall
with Daddy, Daddy, Daddy.

Greek and Roman statues
        Faun carrying Bacchus

          the poet Euripides
              resting Satyr, half goat, half man
all staring down
from their perches near the ceiling
on
all of us
staring at the stage
swaying to the sounds of
dulcet violins.

in particular
one very naked plaster cast of a
very naked man
distracting me
from Beethoven, Beethoven, Bee
                            t
                            h
                             o
                             v
                             e
                              n.

# Control Tower

*1950 to 1965*

*Sharon, Massachusetts*

## Chapter one

in sixth grade after school
I made thumbprint butter cookies
little round mounds of yellowy dough
a teaspoon of apricot or raspberry jam
plopped into the depression
the leftover egg whites
whipped up into pointy meringue cookies
freckled with bits of chocolate
a sweet buttery fragrance
anointing the kitchen.

I planned to open a bakery
someday in grownup land
I was a busy aspirational child
good, responsible
unusually mature
proud of that
a real mother-pleaser
without a whole lot of friends.
(I think she liked it that way;
I was hers)

I grew up in
a yet-to-be-discovered
little town
south of Boston
juiced by neighborly gossip
and good cheer.

fleeing Brooklyn
my mother had read Thoreau's
*Walden Pond* and yearned for
an old New England village

with a lake, lush forests
frosty autumnal air
imbued with transcendentalism and philosophy.

an antidote to the coarseness and tumble
of shtetl Brooklyn, New York.

Sharon boasted
Lake Massapoag
a bounty of trees
an Audubon Society
bells in the Unitarian and Congregational Churches
forged by Paul Revere
a town heroine, Deborah Sampson
disguised as a man
fought in the Revolutionary War
worked a farm with clucking chickens
that still clucked just up the hill
from our one-and-a-half wooded acres.

on July 4th
paunchy vets from two World Wars
and Korea
marched proudly down Main Street
behind screaming red fire engines
hand-waving town selectman
the Knights of Columbus.

> my family perched on wooden fences
> on the edge of our
> optometrist's lawn
> waving our flags
> slurping watermelon
> sticking our tongues into
> sickly sweet pink wisps of cotton candy
> like real Americans.

it was a cozy, safe, small, white place.

## Chapter two

I was my mother's
best friend good girl helper bunny
absorbing her smarts and apprehensions
her anxiety over her upward mobility
as she glided into the Protestant landscape
her worries about *Jewish continuity*
a catchword in liberal postwar America.

that yearning to be
separate, distinctive
a member of the cultured
Jewish intelligentsia
(not the ghettoed community
of immigrant parents)
but not so goyish
the children would marry
god forbid
a gentile.

I came to understand
our family was different
superior
more creative and successful
than the rest
piano lessons
ballet lessons
violin lessons.

art classes up a nondescript
winding stairway
off the gift shop in the
Museum of Fine Arts.

my sister studied flute
my brother, viola
we were busy productive
mostly willing children.

                    my mother's
                attitudes were born of
                  accomplishment
                     arrogance
                     insecurity
               her own deeply disturbing
                    narcissism
                a mind-fuck of a message
                 a lonely place to be
               in a small-minded town.

memory:
many years later I was
invited to give a lecture
at Harvard Medical School
a continuing medical education course
for a group of social workers and psychiatrists
The Impact Of Hormones On Female Mood And Emotion
(or something like that)
I spent weeks preparing
invited my mother
to see me in action.
(I thought she would be proud, happy)

after the lecture I was swarmed
by eager interested therapists
wanting to talk
with me
I introduced my mother
(wanting her to feel comfortable, welcomed
to share in my success)
within seconds, she began enchanting the crowd
smart, entertaining, witty
the entire group turned away from me
towards her.

moths fluttering to the brightest light.

I was left standing alone
small
invisible

my anger and resentment
tempered by the knowledge that
my mother could not tolerate
not being the center of attention.

especially when I was.

we had danced this dance before
but now I understood it
with crushing clarity.

my mother aspired
to be a cultured person
there was no yelling in our house
*we were better than that*
(and little disagreement)
she loved playing her cello
(in and out of tune)
with the local civic orchestra
painting oils of fiddlehead ferns
beach scenes from Cape Cod
a canvas of giant angry red swirls.
(a blast of emotion after her
hysterectomy un-sexed her
in ways I can only conjecture)

it looked almost perfect
but nothing ever is.

## Chapter three

my mother guarded her children fiercely
with a jumble of double messages
defiance
self-doubt.

                                   baked a chicken every Friday
                                   blessed Shabbos candles

but rarely went to synagogue.

                                   sent me to Hebrew school
                                   three times a week
                                   to be a literate
                                   knowledgeable Jew
                                   grounded in my inheritance

but only spoke Yiddish
when she wanted to say something
I shouldn't understand.

                                   I always wondered why
                                   her need to assimilate
                                   prevailed.

                                   why she
                                   severed me from
                                   the mother-tongue
                                   that could have been
                                   an emotional cement
                                   a link to
                                   Eastern European culture
                                   immigrant relations
                                   a sprawl of cousins.

she was proud of her liberalism
hosted a young John F. Kennedy
at a gathering on our lawn
during a Senate race in the 1950s.

supported Adlai Stevenson for President in 1956
                          while gangs of mean-spirited girls at school
                                  chanted *we hate Adlai very badly*

and kicked me in my shins
to make their point.

(those liberal minded Jews moving in
threatening *our*
quiet steepled town)

I grew up like a wild pony
contained by an invisible electrified fence
marking the limits of
my choices and behavior.

I lived by her rules
which were strict but unspoken
the boundaries of my freedom only discovered
when I vaulted against her edges
jolted by a bolt of electrical condemnation.
(we had no language
for disagreement
or discontent
her and me)

## Chapter four

I was her pride, her legacy
tacitly mired in her love
jealousy
competitiveness
insecurity
(she would have denied all)
I never developed
the skills
of argument.
(except fortress construction
and silence
which I learned
from my father)

mom always said
he did learn to talk.

I always wondered
when was that?

memory:

my parents are snuggled on the couch
smooching on and off
drinks in hand
Tchaikovsky booming from the record player
my little sister and I are dancing
baby brother standing on a chair
conducting the symphony.

I wonder if even then I understood
his boy job was to be in charge
I could be *anything you want sweetheart*
as long as there was a man
(Jewish, doctor, lawyer)
who made the money
took charge
and I put the children first

but then, after that
*anything darling anything.*

memory:

we are traipsing through
grassy bogs on Cape Cod
salty air on our tongues
feet gritty with sand
we come to a small bridge
over a tidal stream
my mother panics
unable to cross
her fear of heights
paralyzing her
my father responds
teasing her
belittling
taunting
as she heroically
inches across.

I watch her man
shaming her
knowing
that can't be right.

memory:

my mother always
dieting
melba toast standing guard
daddy with his comments and jokes
about the size of her butt.
(he would have denied all)

I wonder then
did he love her
as she was?
(I understood the marriage
improved)
but was he kind?

did she live in fear
of losing him?
(handsome, successful, gracious with the ladies)

did I fill some void
some lack of intimacy and trust
in her 1950s marriage?

# Chapter five

by my teens
she prided in our
intimate relationship.
(no teenage rebellion for her
almost perfect daughter)

painfully lonely
but accomplished, striving
I sometimes felt like
a prized race horse
galloping around the track
top speed
no exit.

waiting at the bus stop
in my bobby socks
clunky tie shoes
clutching my violin
straight "A"s
back when nerdiness
was a character flaw
to be avoided
the other girls clustered
away from me.

is that when I realized
I would never be
good enough
desirable enough
acceptable enough
perfect enough
or was that just
the state of
being female?

when I finally left home
desperate to chart

my own flight path
I discovered I had the skills to fly.

but my mother was still
in the control tower.

# People Said We Were a Perfect Family

*1948 onward*

*Everywhere*

## Musings

at first I thought
my mother was a towering pine
cradling me in soft needles
offering boughs
to climb.

I stare up at her
half-naked on my baby blanket
tongue tipped toward nose
dimple fisted
thunder thighs
the cloth
emblazoned with a blue flag
ALICE
in swirly letters
total adoration.

on second thought
maybe a maple tree
better to scramble up
sweet syrup in her veins
leaves turning brilliant scarlet
in the fall
crunchy piles good for jumping off
into the world
emerald green shoots reborn in the spring
everlasting.

school musical
fifth grade
I get the lead part
because I can sing and
whistle reliably

when the magic tree
(Herman Steinberg)
grants me a wish

and I'm not
shy.

best of all
I get a new dress
COVERED WITH RED ROSES.

I play the part of
Melody, the new girl in town
accused of being a witch
rescued by Johnny Appleseed.
(but plagued by magic seeds)

Mom beams from the front row
of the high school auditorium
flanked by my sister and brother
she's channeling
we got this
youandme.

one tortured day
I discovered my mother
was part beach rose
a ThOrN bUsH
pricking my face
my arms
my heart
if I twisted
in
the
wrong
direction.

## Mother/daughter

there is a benefit
and a risk
to having a mother
who is a writer.

I can stare
deep into the
well of her feelings
(unfiltered)
through her own written word.

I came to know her by lines like this:

*Hadassah Magazine*
Parenting Section.
a story I suspect she thought
        poignant
                sweet
                        ironic
                                humorous.

about her grandchildren
why she wanted to be called
*bubbe.*

an ode to old-fashioned love
the memories and myths of her Yiddish-speaking childhood.

tucked into the seductive charm
was everything that made me
CrAzY

quote:

> *We had been*
> *one of those close warm families*
> *in which children are slow to rebel,*
> *having too little cause.*
> *Their separations came from*
> *visceral rather than rational conflicts*

*in an atmosphere of contrived*
*and causeless*
*hostility.*
*Late marriages and pregnancies*
*delayed the end of the*
*mishegas.*
[translation: Yiddish, insanity]

even now
lines like that
push my RAGE BUTTON
a frustrating
        hurtful
                endless struggle
with my long-dead mother.

like many who grew up
in an actual family
I had my share of complaints
        years of distrust
                disillusionment.

as did she.

I built a fortress of silence
for my own survival
and sanity.

she built a fortress
of resentment
and disappointment.

she was better at angry.
I was better at mute
smiling when socially required.

in my early thirties
married and finally recognizably
respectable
I invited her
to be part of my first pregnancy.

        a gift.

gave her time with her grandchildren.

a shared treasure.

that did not mean I trusted her.

her capacity to feel blameless
when it came to me
poisoned our relationship.

a mother unable to own
          her share of the bargain
                    who belittles
                              mine.

decades later
I still pull out the thorns
one
by
one
rubbing my bruised skin
          trying to find a path

                    towards forgiveness.

## Assassinations in Two Parts

*1963 to 1968*

*United States of America*

### Part one

Friday, November 22, 1963
forty-six-year-old President John F. Kennedy
finished his speech
at the Fort Worth Chamber of Commerce breakfast
probably ran a comb
through his thick chestnut hair
adjusted his tie
took the hand of his elegant wife Jacqueline
boarded a plane for the short flight to
Dallas's Love Field airport.

a bright balmy day
he shook hands with a congenial crowd
climbed into the back seat
of a classy, black, customized open convertible
an American flag drooping from the right front grill
slid in next to his wife
all pearls, white gloves
a pink pill box hat
maybe commented on the sunny weather
the enthusiastic throngs
the brace he always wore
his ever-present back pain.

(an old football injury
the ramming of his PT boat
by a Japanese destroyer
World War II
four unsuccessful back surgeries
a brace that held him ramrod straight)
an easy target.

Democratic Texas Governor John Connally and his wife
joined them in jump seats in front
with a motorcycle escort
secret service on foot.

some 200,000 patriotic flag-waving people
lined the ten mile route
desperate to catch a glimpse
of the privileged, handsome, young
silver-tongued president.

on the edge of downtown Dallas
the motorcade turned southwest
on Elm Street
crossing through Dealey Plaza
past the Texas School Book Depository.

that morning
almost 2,000 miles away
I sat in ninth grade biology class
rows of students at individual wooden-topped desks
heads bent
taking notes.

I can't remember what the teacher
was saying
maybe I was listening
or worrying about a French test
the unacceptable state of my unruly hair
how tired I felt
sleeping on three inch rollers
would my new violin teacher
like my arpeggios?

it was an ordinary wintry morning
I was looking forward to my birthday.

the intercom clicked
heads popped up
eyed the brown box
mounted on the wall

the principal's deep scratchy voice
filled the classroom.

> *President Kennedy has been shot.*
> *Return immediately to your homerooms.*
> *School will be dismissed shortly.*

a shock wave shook the class
my heart hammered
how could this be?
assassins?
a coup?
in America?
in 1963?

students clustered on the sidewalk
in front of the school
crying, fearful
girls hugged each other.

by the time the bus dropped me off at home
he was dead.

I huddled with my mother and siblings
transfixed by the scenes
on our black and white television
CBS
*As The World Turns*
ads for a new minute brew Nescafe
repeatedly interrupted
by News Bulletin
until they went to
full coverage.

Walter Cronkite's level, authoritative voice
clipped, just-the-facts-as-we-see-them delivery
seated in a jumble of black dial phones
mounting piles of paper updates
thick black glasses, tired baggy eyes
formal white shirt, dark tie
frenzied men jumping in and out of the screen.

*Let us recount this incident again . . .*
*Bullet wounds into his chest . . .*
*Cut down . . .*
*Priests have been called to Parkland Hospital . . .*

my sense of order
jolted into chaos and confusion.

my first televised catastrophe
visuals seared into my memory
as if altering my very DNA
Jackie in her pale jacket and skirt
smeared with her husband's blood and fragments of brain
bullet casings near a window on the sixth floor
of the Texas School Book Depository
Lyndon Johnson's grim swearing in
aboard Air Force One
the mournful set of Jackie's jaw
disbelief in her eyes.

the arrest of Lee Harvey Oswald
in the back of a dark movie theater
a caisson bearing the flag-draped coffin
pulled by six white horses
followed by the black riderless horse
backward boots hanging in the stirrups.

two days later, on my birthday
still drifting in a fog of national mourning and uncertainty
I was ironing sheets, pillow cases
piles of my father's boxer shorts, cloth dinner napkins
blouses, skirts, trousers
(my mother paid by the piece)
in my basement
riveted to an old TV.

at 10:21 am, Oswald appeared
for his transfer
city jail to county jail
bland puckish face
security men in loose suits and ties

firmly grasped his arms
in the basement of the Dallas Police Department Headquarters.

Jack Ruby, a pudgy, dimple-chinned
Dallas nightclub owner
who dabbled in illegal gambling, narcotics, prostitution
lunged out of nowhere
drew a small caliber pistol
shot Oswald point blank in the stomach
face grimacing, recoiling
as he clutched his tortured abdomen
on live TV.

in front of me.

in my basement.

at my ironing board.

I ran upstairs
yelling MOM.

until then, my awareness
of national disaster
political realities
had been pretty sketchy.

democracy was a settled kind of thing
with a few loose ends around the Negro Problem
anti-Semitism
nuclear war
unspoiled American myths were Real
the Vietnam War, just beginning to loom
into public consciousness.

in my mind
presidents didn't get killed in the twentieth century.

deranged bad actors with a grudge and a gun?
CIA?
mafia?
police?
Guzanos (angry anti-Castro Cubans)?

a web of deep-state conspiracies?
an ominous right-wing ascendency?
didn't really matter to me
until
now.

my naïve (middle class, white) understanding
about the neatness
and predictability of things
had been

shattered.

## Part two

five years later, Martin Luther King Jr
traveled to Memphis Tennessee
to support striking African American city sanitation workers.

already caused a fuss
publicly declaring his opposition to the Vietnam War
organizing the Poor People's Campaign
talking about radical political change.

after years of death threats
his prophetic *I've Been to the Mountaintop* speech
he leaned over a balcony railing in front of room 306
at the Lorraine Motel
said something to Reverend Jesse Jackson.

a shot exploded.

King crumpled backwards
a single bullet to the face
fired by James Earl Ray
in a rooming house across the street.

by then I was in college
more educated, more involved
in the struggle for racial justice
not that surprised
but utterly horrified and outraged.

two months later, JFK's
forty-two-year-old brother
Senator Robert Kennedy
campaigning for the Democratic presidential primary
exited through a kitchen hallway
after a campaign celebration

assassinated at the Ambassador Hotel
Los Angeles.

twenty-four-year-old
Sirhan Sirhan fired multiple shots

at close range
(more debate about a second shooter, a conspiracy . . .)
captured on audiotape and film.

I was a college sophomore
buried in premed chemistry/physics/science labs
no longer surprised

by white supremacy, gun violence, racism, death.

# PART THREE: BATTLEFIELD

In which the battle lines for love and medicine are drawn.

# On the Cusp

*1966*

*Brookline, Massachusetts & Bryn Mawr College*

*Bryn Mawr, Pennsylvania*

that spring
we moved to Brookline
upscale
first Jewish family in the neighborhood.

one morning I marched down the stairs
in blue jeans
a tee shirt
(mom didn't let me wear pants in public
too slutty but
home was okay)
whistling
sliding my hand
on the railing
like warm butter
on a hot corn cob.

a middle-aged electrician
strode through
the front door
of my parents' just-bought colonial
brick house
looked me
up
and
down
my body framed by the
the curved wooden banister.

his face crumpled in a
scowl.
            *Ladies don't whistle.*

impertinent
blurt.

> *I'm not a lady.*

that summer
my daddy "taught" me to drive
in rush-hour city traffic
using the what-doesn't-kill-you-makes-you-stronger
method of instruction
he reckoned I would just
figure it out.
(hopefully without running over too many small children)

I powered us home
(and him to a stiff gin and tonic)
at the end of each afternoon
from my dreadfully tedious shipping clerk job
at his company.

white-knuckled, dry-mouthed
fiercely determined to master this grownup trick.

months later
first year of college
where we signed out of the dorm
in the evenings
and couldn't
legally
have
a man
or booze
in our rooms.

I lived by the rules
(still figuring it out)
voted against
wearing pants
to class
convinced that was

> Disrespectful to the Professors.

thankfully, that opinion
didn't last
very long.

## Transgression

*1967*

*Brookline, Massachusetts*

clothes half-on
half-off
like petals strewn across the back seat
in a flail of delight
the hunger of ardent kisses
warm tongues
eager fingers.

his parent's car
tucked into the leafy darkness
of a town park.

a blinding flashlight
exploded into our private space
as I grabbed for my shirt
two cops peered
ghoul-eyed
through the window.

      panic.

      terror.

      white girl in the arms of
      black boy.

would the Irish cops
demand a piece of me
slutty girl in a car
beat him
arrest him
or worse
for daring to touch
me
white girl
trashy white girl

drag us back
sirens blaring
to our disapproving parents?

no breath
pulse pounding in my temples
mouth as dry as menaced desire.

one cop bellowed

*Get your clothes on.*
*Get out of here.*

the other snickered

*Try the parks in Boston.*
*Less patrols.*

## Bewitched by Love

*1966 to 1969*

*Cambridge, Massachusetts*

our plans were all dreams and serious purpose
a life braided together
we would go to medical school
train in psychiatry
two head-shrinkers
maybe share an office.

our children, smart and good-looking
our home, alive with Brahms and Prokofiev
thick, important books.

he wrote me lyrical poetry
filled with ardor and yearning
a young man desperate for loving
pursuing his hopes
in that ivy-covered Harvard dorm
a single bed, green-blue plaid cover
roommates to be avoided
two virgins
figuring it out.

I was bewitched by love
but so desperately afraid of pregnancy
I have no memories
(except his manhood felt like velvet)
of the details.

there was always a condom
we were sensible.

*New York legalized abortion 1970*
*Roe v Wade, 1973.*

this was all before that.
I was scared every time.

my mother once told me
she would know
if I was *doing it.*

coming home from the dorm
I stood brazenly in front of her
realized
She Doesn't Know.

when she discovered
we were *serious*
that I intended to marry this Black Man
this Harvard man
this soloist with the Boston Symphony Orchestra
with incredible smarts, a sweet disposition, good looks
the punishment was swift.

she threatened to sit shiva
the ritual of mourning
for the dead.

to cast me out
because he was not a Nice Jewish Boy
[And He Was Black.]

> *Think of what you will lose!*

she wept
never imagining that he stood to lose as well
me
a white woman.

> *US Supreme Court, Loving v Virginia, 1967*
> *laws banning interracial marriage*
> *violate the Constitution.*

that all happened while we were
embracing, hoping, believing, imagining
our skin to soft silky skin.

this was the moment
I first understood
my mother was not to be trusted

all her liberal Democratic Party
Adlai Stevenson John F. Kennedy civil rights tolerance
was of no use
in the face of trauma and tribalism.

*If you marry a non-Jew*
*Hitler's dream will come true.*

[And He's Black.]

we went underground
secret lovers
but didn't last for more mundane reasons
colleges 300 miles away
growing up
and apart.

mostly, he reminded me of my father
smart, talented, emotionally disconnected.

I wanted a different life.
I had seen that show before.

I summoned my courage
and

left.

# Only Our Failures Get Married

*1966 to 1970*

*Bryn Mawr College*

*Bryn Mawr, Pennsylvania*

I arrived early
for my first day of college
which officially started on
the Jewish New Year
which I spent in some cavernous suburban Philadelphia temple
while my soon-to-be classmates
        chatted
                drank tea
                        nibbled crustless cucumber sandwiches.

the college was built in 1885
to provide women with a rigorous education
equal to men
white-gloved Quaker ladies
with smarts, ambition
and a yearning for graduate degrees.

at the college they used to say

        *Only our failures get married.*

that's actually debatable -
the quote may have been

        *Our failures only marry.*

attributed to a M. Carey Thomas
suffragist, linguist
first dean and second president
back when lesbianism was not mentioned
in polite society
women like her
lived with their "partners" or "companions."

back when Jewish students and faculty
were turned away
in favor of
*our own good Anglo-Saxon stock.*
(according to the otherwise forward-thinking
M. Carey)

Pembroke West was a grey castle of a dorm
with turrets, arched windows
crenellations and battlements
a Gothic Victorian fortress
the archway
flanked by stone lions
bearing shields decorated
with symbols of Pallas Athena
Greek goddess of warfare and wisdom.

Katherine Hepburn lived there
Class of 1928.

we sang hymns to the goddess
in the medieval cloisters of the library
wearing academic regalia
holding colored lanterns flickering with candle light.

> *Sophias, philai, paromen,*
> *Philokaloumen met euteleias*
> (Friends of wisdom, let us gather,
> We love beauty with simplicity)

watched the sunrise
in white dresses
    ate strawberries and cream
        sipped champagne in fluted glasses
            rolled wooden hoops
                danced around ribboned poles
on May Day
on Merion Green.

> *To the maypole let us on*
> *The time is swift and will be gone*
> *Then come lasses to the green*

*Where their beauties may be seen . . .*
*Come together, come sweet lass,*
*Let us trip it on the grass.*

the room next to my bedroom
was a tiny closet
built for the student's maid back when
        students had maids
but now assigned
        to a girl on scholarship.

I felt like an intruder
        public school
                Jewish
the daughter of a striving father
who made it on his own dreams
and the GI bill
his father, an immigrant shopkeeper

        *J. Rothchild*
        *Russian & Turkish*
        *Tobacco.*

the what-to-bring-to-college list
included a tea set.
        (no fancy china bequeathed by my
        Yiddish-speaking
        illiterate
        grandmama)

My *bubbe* shared a bed with
        her sisters
                chickens cackling
                        dirt floor
in a tiny village *shtetl*
in the Austro-Hungarian Empire
Carpathian Mountains.

a different kind of inheritance.

tea time was 4:00 p.m.

I found my way
amidst the dark, wood-trimmed halls
        many paned lead windows
                gargoyles and arches
mingled with daughters of ambassadors
women with legacies
winter break ski trips to Switzerland
subscriptions to the Philadelphia Orchestra.

women who majored in art history, archeology
took the enviable junior year abroad
to Spain or France.

a student once asked shyly

>       *May I touch you?*
>       *I've never met a Jew before.*

in the dining hall
with its high ceiling
massive stone fireplaces
carvings in Latin
something like *veritatem dilexi.*
        (which, as a science major
        I translated roughly
        *the truth is delicious*)

we sat in high-backed chairs
at long dark tables
served by Black women
in crisp grey uniforms
        with starched white collars
                and aprons
the private school girls
ate bananas with a knife
and didn't leave crumbs.

there were twelve Black women
in my class of one hundred twenty.

a generously built African American woman
sat all day in a booth

just past the living room
across from the *smoker*
taking messages
monitoring our behavior.

this almost totally white campus
drenched in upper-crust traditions
served by African American *help*
felt deep south
almost *Gone with the Wind.*

my first uneasy collision
with class and race.

## Reading Between the Lines

*1966*

*Bryn Mawr College*

*Bryn Mawr, Pennsylvania*

LETTERS FROM MY MOTHER
Wednesday
Dearest,
Just received your letter.
The mailman insisted it was too heavy—
asked for an extra nickel.
Actually it was not a question of weight—
it was that poem, worth lots and lots of nickels—
maybe the best you ever wrote.
Send it somewhere—
with my blessing.
I don't know what I'd do if you belonged to someone else—
I'd die of jealousy.

> thanks Mom.
> love you too.
> you're my best best friend.

Love the way you're meeting the world, head on—
It's the only way—
Later on—There'll be time for modesty shyness, etc.
The race at the moment is to the "warm, glamorous, sexy."

> wait? what?
> Mom, you want me to be
> sexy???

But why should I tell you—you know everything—
all I can say is that you're absolutely right.
*Yasher koach* . . .
[Yiddish: May it be for strength . . .
congratulations, good job]

> actually Mom
> I'm a smart
> somewhat terrified
> teenager

away from home for the first time
never been in a serious relationship
desperately hoping to get into medical school
while gazillions of guys are applying
to stay out of Vietnam
with a medical deferment.

do you really know me?
Great that you can play in that pro-training orchestra.
You'll have daddy playing second fiddle for you yet.

in my dreams
he isn't about to give up
playing first violin
to his

daughter.

Tuesday . . . big snow . . . no school

Dear Alice
Got your personal-private letter yesterday. . . .
Heaved a deep sigh . . .
where to begin?

must have asked her
about sex.

I know that when someone very special reaches you
you will not ask me or tell me . . .
even good daughter that you are.
So it's especially important to talk
when talking is still possible.

true.

In a time when everything is relative . . .
it's good to remember that in Judaism . . .
to sin . . . has nothing to do
with hell and damnation . . .
but is a way of saying . . .
that is a mistake . . .
an unfortunate choice.
It is also important to remember
that actions are not bad because they are sinful. . . .
they are sinful because they are bad for you.

hold on.
why are we talking about
sin?
you're not a religious person.
I thought we were talking about
sex.

A sexual encounter is like others
except that its effect is to an umpteenth power . . .
When young women are casual about sex,
I have to assume they are unsure enough of their identity
to have nothing to give up . . .

why is this about identity?
what about sexual pleasure?
passion?
curiosity?
love?

Sexual activity . . . like everything else
takes some natural talent and then a lot of practice. . . .
A little bit that is bad . . . can harm . . .

true.

The challenge is for two people
who can take pleasure in giving each other pleasure . . .
this has nothing to do with eager beaver college boys . . .
who know what they want . . .
but cannot know what you need . . .

pretty cynical
possibly true.

Marriage . . . by providing a maximum of
temptation and opportunity
and a long period of time . . .
in an atmosphere of affection and responsibility
is an ideal environment for
discovering sexual possibilities . . .

pretty dreamy
description of marriage, Mom.
didn't you sleep with Dad before?
have you heard the divorce rate
is rising?
women in their 20s

are getting divorced
A LOT.
maybe the traditional
Leave-it-to-Beaver
happy-homemaker
daddy-at-work
kids-bounce-home-for-milk-and-cookies
marriage
is not so great
for women
opportunities to get laid
notwithstanding.

The casual . . . or temporary relationship . . .
offers the worst . . .
the most anxiety . . .
the least satisfaction (for girls) . . .

what are you saying?
boys don't feel pain?
girls aren't satisfied?

And then the pain when it is over . . .
and meaningless.
What girls don't realize is the new freedom . . .
frees them to behave like boys . . .

you mean like your husband?
your son?
some random frat boy?

To pretend . . . that they [girls] are untouched, unreached . . .
that they can thrive on casual relationships. . . .
When in fact they want to marry
most of the boys they get involved with . . .

don't think so.

Or else despise themselves for getting involved
so intimately with people
that they couldn't stand for more than a night or two.

you've lost me here.

There is no doubt in my mind . . .
that you'll have more
if you can wait . . .
I would like to know . . . about these girls who chose to be freer . . .

what kind of parents they have,
what kind of marriages they've seen,
what they want to do with their lives . . .

now we get to the
We're Better Than That
Theory of being a Rothchild
not like those other girls
with inadequate parents
unhappy marriages
free of meaning and dreams.

not like us.

The verdict in this department
gotten from Babee [her mother]
who got it from Alice [her grandmother]

stop.

Babee never married her first love
took a husband who claimed her
because she was next in line
in a big family of girls.

Alice was married young
probably arranged by her parents
lived in a rural shtetl
in Eastern Europe
a good orthodox Jewish wife.
and these are your experts on
premarital sex????

*The later the sun comes up, the nicer the day will be.*
I hated to hear about it when I was eighteen
because I was afraid it was true . . .
now I know it is.

did you get burned?
not the story you told me.

From the other end of the cord,

she's talking umbilical cord.
cute.
no boundaries whatsoever.

Much love,
Mama

Also do those other girls have any music, art, etc.
to pour their feelings into . . .
                                    Back to our superiority
                                         as cultured
                                           creative
                                            people
                                      who sublimate
                                       sexual urges
                                    until the big day.
Later when they have every night of their life to sleep with someone
(How tame it sounds when it's legal) . . .
there will be no time for cultivating and development of Self . . .
this is the big and only chance for most of them . . .
If they give it up. . . .
it's because they're chicken . . .
You can't listen to yourself . . .
and to man and children.

                                         So you're saying
                           a woman's independent creative
                                          life ends when
                                           she marries?

                                      Was she talking about
                                              herself?

                                       Why would I ever want
                                         to get married?

                                    Free love looks a lot more
                                            liberating
                                               and
                                           satisfying.

## Morphing

*1967*

*Brooklyn, New York*

for months
my New York friend and I planned
The Visit
my first chance to see glittery New York
go to the theater, a show, eat in a chic restaurant
bypass the Jewish ghettos of Brooklyn
and all my (kosher) relatives
who (in my youthful opinion)
lived narrow, incurious lives
of suffering and low expectations.

the day I arrived from Philadelphia
my *zayde* died
a massive snowstorm carpeted the Northeast
as if a major weather event was destined to mark the passing
of this simple, upright man.

showing up at my grandfather's funeral was now
my responsibility
my parents stuck on a train
chugging slowly south
through dense snowdrifts
from Boston.

> *Just like Sylvie*
> *To miss her father's funeral.*

I stepped in
to take her place
sitting in the first black limo behind the hearse
between her two red-eyed sisters
clinging to a page of prayers
and my identity.

at the simple ceremony
uncles and cousins and aunts

who had not seen my mother in decades
had never met me
grabbed my hand, kissed my face, whispered

*Sylvie, you haven't changed a bit.*

who am I?

a college girl defiantly
building fences
trenches
moats
defining my boundaries
testing my options

until I silently morphed into my mother
disappointing no one but
myself.

## Organic Chemistry

*1969*

*Harvard Summer School*

*Cambridge, Massachusetts*

lectures every day
in a deep pit of an amphitheater
where my dreams and self-esteem
were crushed
by the speed learning
of a foreign tongue.

chemical equations cajoled
   carbon
      hydrogen
        nitrogen
          oxygen
            sulfur

  the dance of polarity, acidity, triple bonds
    hieroglyphics of molecules
   honeycombs of carbon chains
   a devastating exam every week
    laboratory most sunny
      summer
     afternoons.

at night I wept
from confusion and exhaustion
never asked my father
the organic chemist
for help.

he didn't offer.

my first lab, my first experiment
exploded
I frantically scrubbed the crystals
off the tall gothic window

scraping my future into a beaker
my grade dependent on my yield
which was evaporating rapidly.

I had been told

> *Organic chemistry is the best predictor*
> *Of how you will perform in medical school.*

my desperation equaled my anxiety
half the class flunked and left
before the eight weeks were over.

those of us who survived or just persisted
mostly got Cs.

> *Not good enough for medical school.*

I was told.

I audited the course
the following two semesters in college
hoping to redeem myself
got an A.
but it didn't count on my transcript.
(failure counting more than success)

> *Don't even bother to apply.*

## Not Quite Right

*1970*

*Bryn Mawr College*

*Bryn Mawr, Pennsylvania*

I loved curly haired energetic Dr Y
took his courses
animal learning, neurophysiology
devoted hours to running pigeons
in his lab

(did you know you can get attached to a pigeon?)

weighing each one
in a cone-shaped contraption
as it cooed and churruped
struggled to move its wings
trapped like a giant grey cannoli

I left jokey notes on their cages

> *Will you still need me?*
> *Will you still feed me?*
> *When I'm 64.*

Dr Y and I published a paper together
like real scientists
so when he invited me and my friend
another psych major
(drop dead gorgeous
and smart)
to his house for
a lovely dinner cooked by
his lovely wife
and we sat on the couch
in front of the lovely appetizers and
glasses of wine
in front of her and he put
his arm around me

on one side
and his arm around
my friend
on the other
and hugged us
tight
       tight
             tight
grinning at his wife

as if he were claiming us
as his
girls

that didn't feel
quite
right
       right
           right.

## Graduation

*May 1970*

*Bryn Mawr College*

*Bryn Mawr, Pennsylvania*

the bell in Taylor Hall
clanged ominously
a protest against the US invasion
of Cambodia.

I marched in my billowing
black robe
ermine hood
white armband.

another mark of rebellion.

in four years
I had joined tens of thousands
rallying against US policies
the sending of young men
in the name of
      ideology
          empire
              capitalism.

decades of fresh faces
shipped off to fight wars in
      Vietnam
          Laos
              Cambodia

to die
      kill civilians
          napalm villages
              poison fields and rice paddies
              (and themselves)
                  with Agent Orange
                     often returning broken, addicted
                     taunted and tormented.

I had labored over
my honors thesis
analyzed rat behavior
the effect of
neurochemicals
dropped into a spot
in the hypothalamus
through tiny tubes
I implanted in their brains.

collected data
          prepared pathology slides
                    struggled through statistical analyses
                              wrote and rewrote that paper

until my advisor was
fully
satisfied.

I had just performed
the Dvorak piano quintet
in A major
Allegro, Dumka, Scherzo
(parents beaming)
after a year of rehearsals
hours of violin
          practice
                    practice
                              practice
stretching beyond my imagination
with four other students
equally determined and inspired.

I had finally
gotten into medical school
(all you need is one)
wait-listed at two.

I stood on the grassy rolling hills
neatly clipped lawns
stately grey stone buildings

surrounded by a roiling river of
smart
accomplished
privileged women.

a swarm of bees
leaving the nest.

the world a deeply uncertain
unwelcoming place.

## THE FACTS

in 1970
banks could require a woman
applying for credit
have her husband co-sign.

in 1970
employers could legally fire
a woman for being pregnant.

in 1970
conjugal rights meant
that it was legal for a man
to rape
his wife.

US laws included
housing discrimination
pay discrimination
jury exclusion
for women.

a husband had
unilateral control
of property
jointly owned.

a woman had half the legal rights of a man
earned fifty-nine cents to the dollar.

help-wanted ads in newspapers
listed jobs separately
for men
(just about everything)
for women
(secretarial, nursing, teaching)
in 1970.

the swarm buzzed and swooped
on the cusp
of a new world
the frenetic
winged flight
blossom to blossom.

sucking up nectar
breaking it down
the constant fanning of wings
evaporating liquid
creating a sweet golden liquor
to nurture the young.

constructing a life of hard work.

stinging when provoked.

my class
a murder of crows
swooping out of a pine tree
to dive bomb a predator.

an avalanche of rock
tumbling down a mountain
making a new path.

a sisterhood
forged in protest
        outrage
                ambition.

twenty-five years later
Supreme Court Justice
Ruth Bader Ginsburg said:

*I ask no favor for my sex.*
*All I ask of our brethren is that*
*they take their feet off our necks.*

# Kent State Massacre: Kids Like Us

*1970s*

*USA, Vietnam, Laos, Cambodia*

*I covered the Vietnam War. I remember the lies that were told, the lives that were lost—and the shock when, twenty years after the war ended, former Defense Secretary Robert S. McNamara admitted he knew it was a mistake all along.*
*Walter Cronkite*
*CBS Evening News anchor 1962-1981*

US college students
(even at Bryn Mawr
with its Garden Parties and Flower Girls)
were out in the streets
organizing
      leafleting
           protesting.

lobbying congress
      calling elected officials
           sending telegrams
                  15 words for 95 cents.

striking
(we had a Strike Committee and a candle light march
to the draft board in the town of Bryn Mawr)
occupying buildings
      knocking on doors
           canvassing
                raising funds.
                (an elderly lady gave me her treasured possession
                a delicately beaded purse
                asked me to sell it
                donate the money for peace)

young men burned their draft cards
faced indictments, prison time
fled to Canada to avoid conscription.

hundreds of thousands of angry hopeful disillusioned people
determined to stop
*young men fighting old men's wars*
making the links between
militarism
        liberation,
                self-determination.

                              brooding
                              secretive
                              conspiratorial
                    President Richard Nixon
                    called anti-war protestors
                              on US campuses
                              *bums*
                    *communist pawns.*

        (the US already covertly bombing Laos and Cambodia)

                    gaffe-ridden Vice President Spiro Agnew
                                       told his boss
                              *stop pussyfooting around.*

                    not exactly quality leadership
             at the helm of the military-industrial complex.

April 28, 1970
US ground troops invaded
while B-52 bombers dropped their deadly cargo on
North Vietnamese bases and bodies
in eastern Cambodia.

May 1
500 students at Kent State protested the invasion
around midnight, people leaving a bar
threw beer bottles
broke windows downtown
the crowd grew, alcohol mixed with outrage.

the mayor called in the entire Kent police force
officers from surrounding towns.

the mayor called a state of emergency
the officers tear gassed the crowd.
(choking, eyes burning, tears flowing, crying)

May 2
protest in front of the ROTC building
a small structure set on fire
demonstrators threw rocks, slashed a fire hose
rampant (false) rumors:
>   students planned to burn businesses, the ROTC building,
>       the post office
>   students were collecting weapons
>   students plotted to put LSD in the local water supply.

the mayor called in the Ohio National Guard
who arrested, tear gassed, bayonetted
students.

May 3
the governor called protesters
>   worse than brown shirts
>       communists
>           vigilantes
>               *They are not going to take over [the]*
>                   *campus.*
>               *I think that we're up against the*
>                   *strongest, well-trained, militant,*
>                   *revolutionary group that has ever*
>                   *assembled in America.*

curfew was called.

students broke curfew
>   called a rally
>       a sit-in.

national guard charged
>   tear gassed
>       chased, bayonetted students
>           helicopters buzzed overhead
>               shining bright spotlights on the
>                   scattering crowd.

May 4
2,000 (mostly) students rallied at noon
rang the iron Victory Bell.
(historically reserved for football games)

ordered to disperse.

national guard fired tear gas
some protestors tossed the canisters back
hurled stones
crowds chanted "Pigs off campus!"
retreated up and over Blanket Hill.

abruptly

a burst of
ta-ta-ta-ta-ta-ta-ta-ta-tat.

                                    28 of the 77 guardsmen
                                        fired their weapons
                                              67 rounds
                                                 in 13
                                               seconds
                                    four students murdered
                                           nine wounded.

the electrifying photo
echoed in my consciousness
        surprise
             horror
                  dread
                       rumbled
                            awakening me like
                                shudders from
                                    an unexpected
                                        earthquake
                                            shattering
                                                glass.

Mary Ann Vecchio
kneeled
hands outstretched

mouth wide open
screamed over a dead body
lying in the street
face down
Jeffrey Miller
(white kids like us)
shot by the National Guard
Kent State.

were they ordered to shoot?
were they (these kids like us) afraid for their lives?
were they trigger happy, fed up, angry, remorseful?

the war had come home
and they were willing to kill us
every campus now a potential battlefield.

Nixon blamed
the (unarmed) students
for resorting to violence.

the killings provoked protests on campuses
throughout the US
millions of students walked out
at hundreds of universities
        colleges
        high schools
450 campuses closed.

100,000 people demonstrated in Washington DC
        uplifting their voices against the war
                against the killing of unarmed protesters.

May 5
Gallup Poll
58% of respondents blamed
the students.

May 15
Jackson State College
city and state police
killed two Black students

injured twelve
no ambulances were called
until the officers finished
collecting their
shell casings.

> 1973—pleading no contest
> to a single felony charge
> of tax evasion
> Agnew resigned
> burying the other charges of
> criminal conspiracy
> bribery
> extortion.

> 1974—facing Watergate and impeachment
> Nixon resigned.

> leaving the helm
> of the shameless lethally armed
> extremely profitable
> military-industrial complex
> to Gerald Ford
> Donald Rumsfeld
> Dick Cheney
> Henry Kissinger.

1975
Vietnam War ended
7,000,000 tons of bombs
twice the amount unleashed on
Europe and Asia
during World War II.

58,200 US troops
1,100,000 million Viet Cong and North Vietnamese fighters
2,000,000 civilians
(mothers fathers children like us)

dead
dead
dead.

# Getting In

*May 1970*

*Boston, Massachusetts*

my acceptance off the wait-list
was a favor from
a friend of the family
on the admissions committee
who offered to
help.

the day after college graduation
the thick envelope arrived
tumbling me off the wait-list
into the unlocked grip of Boston University.

knowing
during this time of the Vietnam War
frenzied competition to avoid the draft
thousands of men applying
to medical school
to stay out of the rice paddies
away from napalm
Agent Orange
the mutilation
gang raping
murdering
massacre
at My Lai
secret bombings in Cambodia
body bags with their bloodied battered cargo
young lives extinguished
away away from all of these things.

I was considered a
*high risk candidate*
(taking the place of a useful male)
with my C in organic chemistry
my D in chem/phys

(a crushing experimental course
I barely survived)
nearly taken down by the firing squad
of pre-med requirements.

a greying psychiatrist
well-established, self-satisfied
enjoyed a nice gin and tonic
a scoop of my mother's famous chopped liver
lovely dinners under my parents' crystal chandelier.

he let me know.

he took a chance on me.

> better not disappoint
> better not cause trouble
> better be good enough.

Good enough!
Good Enough!

he died shortly thereafter
during cardiac bypass surgery.

I always knew
he was heartless.

# Python Love

*1969 to 1970*

*Boston, Massachusetts*

the brash, gin drinking psychologist with the motorcycle
twelve years my senior
divorced
called me his *little virgin*
sent voluptuous bouquets of roses
to my college dorm.

he showed up unannounced
driving from Boston to Philadelphia
in a fit of passion.

he was a cat
stalking me like prey.

renting an apartment
two blocks from my medical school.

tracking down my car
parked in the neighborhood
leaving love notes on the windshield.

meeting me at the end of classes
wrapping his arm around my waist.

claiming me.

my mother called me a whore
told me I'd lost my mind.

which I had.

he was every thing
my Harvard man and my father were not.

wild, unpredictable, fierce, hot-blooded.

leaving him was like
tearing off the jaws
of a python
tightly coiled.

## Trouble

*1970 to 1972*

*Boston University School of Medicine*

*Boston, Massachusetts*

my class was trouble.

the first year of medical school, boot camp.

daily lectures followed by labs
thousands of bits of
Important Facts
about the miraculous human body
its mechanics and chemistry
from ribosomes to ribcages
shoveled into our brains
by professors who mostly preferred to be in the lab.

our very best teacher
sometimes inebriated.

with an exam every week or two
class ranking to the second decimal
we organized a pass/fail system
every student got a number
we each scribbled our number
on each exam
where it said: NAME.

the professors received a decoded list
of who passed and who failed.

they were not happy.

in microbiology
the slides of organs and diseased tissue projected
on the dropdown screen
were interspersed with the occasional
half-naked Playboy Bunny
all boobs and shimmery butts.

many of the guys thought that was funny
the few women and our male accomplices did not.

we went to the Dean
explained how
      demeaning
         sexist
            objectifying
               that felt.

this apparently was news to him
can't we take a joke?

the dedication in my *Williams Obstetrics* textbook
copyright 1971, read:

> *To the men of high purpose who have sometimes*
> *jeopardized their careers in defense of*
> *the right of all children to be well born,*
> *this text is respectfully dedicated.*

women apparently were not that important
when it came to having babies.

the head of obstetrics and gynecology
who actually had a face like a snout
gave the opening lecture of his course

> *What is a woman?*
> *A woman is a man's mother*
> *A man's mistress*
> *A man's competitor*
> ad nauseum.

he used to snort

> *The only good uterus is a uterus on the table.*

HAHAHAHAHA.

provoked, we women rallied outside his lectures
with signs and chants
outraged and disheartened.

we had one session on lesbianism
sat in a darkened auditorium
watched a film
about two women romping through fields of flowers
holding hands, eyeing each other seductively
gently, passionately making love.

this was supposed to *desensitize* us.
       (us being white hetero male)

the second film on gay men
was all bump and grind
erect penises and muscles sweaty
in the heat of the moment
very little else
some men in the class started retching
racing for the doors to vomit.

I don't remember any discussion afterwards.

the American Psychiatric Association
removed homosexuality
as a psychiatric disorder
in 1973.
       (second edition of the
       Diagnostic and Statistical Manual
       of Mental Disorders)

not soon enough.

when the drug company, Eli Lilly
gave each medical student a free stethoscope
       (so we would have warm fuzzy feelings
       towards the pharmaceutical industry
       along with free dinners and other goodies)

we sent our stethoscopes to a medical group in North Vietnam
to protest the US war effort
in solidarity with the napalmed and the maimed.

we wrote a letter of thanks to the drug company
which was published in our local Boston newspaper.

second year
when I came close to failing
the Dean called me in for a chat.

> *What's going on?*
> *Is there a problem?*

how could I tell him
I was drowning in rage
with a good dose of depression
and alienated despair?

## My Cadaver

*1970*

*Boston University School of Medicine*

*Boston, Massachusetts*

her name was Mildred
the hospital band
still crinkled around her wrist
      female
      Catholic.

the first week of medical school
I bent over her slab
in a room reeking of formaldehyde
rows of lumpy bodies lying under sheets
like a giant deadly naptime.

I imagined she used to smell
like lilac
wear pale green sweaters
sensible shoes
a practical woman who donated her body
to science.

or maybe
nobody claimed her
when she died.

first day of anatomy class
a graduate student walked from table to table
slashing each leg.
(the first cut is the hardest)

after that, Mildred felt more like a science project
than a kindly aunt
I once knew
and should not be treated this way.

my dissection partner
a bearded hippy of a man

(with a lawyer for a wife)
had trouble letting me have my turn
with the knife.

I traded him for one of the women
in my class
we propped the text book up on a little shelf
beyond Mildred's greyish toes
delved into a meticulous exploration
>of her muscles
>tendons
>ligaments attached to bone
>joints
>arteries
>veins
>nerves
>heart
>lungs
>kidneys.

our initiation into the brotherhood
the doctorly breaking of boundaries and taboos.

my classmates worked with enthusiasm
only balking when we began
a dissection of the male genitalia.

we women happily did our part.

in the evenings
I compulsively washed my hands
scrubbing off the smells of death
and preservative
dreaming of a fork
with a three foot handle
so I could feed myself
long-distance.

without the dreaded odor
in my face.

## Consciousness Raising

*1970 to 1973*

*various kitchens, living rooms, bedrooms*

*in the Boston area*

college grads
just sorting things out
in a world
made for men
after the wild competitive scramble
to get into medical school.

we were a flock of mismatched birds
flapping as fast as we could
soaring too close to the sun
dive-bombed
by birds of prey
disoriented without a compass
or patterns in the stars
or the pull of the magnetic field.

we swooped, fluttered, nested.

gabbed over hot tea, and mulled cider
spiked with too much red wine
confessed our bewilderment
whispered our outrage
plotted our revenge.

the search for sisters
led us to women
marching in the streets
writing self-help books
*Our Bodies, Ourselves*
plastic speculums, flashlights
shedding light
on the mysteries deep inside.

we searched for a new vocabulary
a radical politic
to guide our way

> feminism
> autonomy
> health—a human right
> patriarchy and privilege
> the avarice of capitalism
> the meaning of consent

the objectification and commodification of our bodies.

the magnetic field tugged
stars shimmered
we noted the terrain and topography
established our migratory flyways.

> a medical student or adult woman patient is not a girl, ever
> do not trust anyone who says
> *don't worry your pretty little head about that*
> or
> *women are so emotional*
> *here's a valium for your*
> PMS, headache, depression, anger.

pick your fights
find your allies
honor your cervix
you know your body better than any doctor.

listen to it.

use those wings.

the index of our obstetrics textbook
had a subversive entry: *male chauvinism*
a secretary added that phrase
and listed all the pages in the book.

> your uterus is the size of a fist.
> (for good reason).

## Sensible Sex

*1970s*

*Boston, Massachusetts*

doctors' offices had displays
of patient education pamphlets
collections of (often demeaning) advice
(outdated) rules of the road
for the female sex and her suitors.

example:

> *One does not take a roast directly from the deep-freeze*
> *and place it in the oven.*
> *It must first be thoroughly*
> *(and sometimes patiently)*
> *thawed out.*

authored by a male doctor
who wrote a syndicated column
"For Women Only"
A Real Expert.

translation:
women (naturally repressed and asexual)
must be
        wooed
                cajoled
                        taught how to respond sexually
                                fake simultaneous orgasms
                                        (he wrote that!)

for the pleasure
of the guy.

he blamed women's *frigidity*
(a common diagnosis then)
on lack of education
            poor *preparation for marriage*
                        unsuccessful encounters

              boredom
                      *anger*
just enough reality to give him
credibility.

He wrote:

       *Men are in a constant state*
       *of sexual readiness.*
       *Women long to be courted.*

his AFTER HYSTERECTOMY WHAT? pamphlet
was funded by a drug company
Beecham-Massengill
with tear off scripts
for their estrogen
on the first page.

goofy sketches of a woman
after a hysterectomy asked

       *Will I become fat and flabby after my hysterectomy?*
       *Will I grow hair on my chin?*
       *Will I become wrinkled, old, masculine, and ugly?*
       *Will I lose all sex desire?*
       *Is it true that some women*
       *lose their minds after a hysterectomy?*

on the discussion of physical activity
after surgery
the ditzy broad was drawn
          climbing stairs
                 cooking
                       driving
                             vacuuming
                                   golfing
female activities.

on the discussion of life opening up to new possibilities
after surgery
the thin white dame wore a flowery hat
banged a gavel

at a podium
for the Ladies Auxiliary League.

such white
        hetero
                middle class
                    silly
                            stupid
                                    sexist

                                        shit.

# Medicalese

*1970 onward*

*Boston Massachusetts & New York, New York*

*pudendal nerve*
carrying sensation
from the vagina and vulva
> from the Latin verb pudere: *to be ashamed.*

*pudendum*
Latin term for the vulva
> *the part to be ashamed of.*

as described in prominent textbooks
> *Gray's Anatomy*
> *Williams Obstetrics*
> *Comprehensive Gynecology.*

words matter.

that infertility patient has an *inadequate luteal phase*
> low levels of progesterone after ovulation
> leading to shortened menstrual cycle.

this miscarriage was caused by an *incompetent cervix*
> the mouth of the uterus does not stay
> tightly closed during pregnancy
> leading to miscarriage
> or premature labor.

the *elderly primipara* is at increased risk for Down syndrome
> a woman 35 or older
> pregnant with her first child
> has a higher rate of
> chromosomal abnormalities
> than younger women.

the dryness and itching is caused by *senile vaginitis*
> vaginal discomfort caused by
> low estrogen levels
> frequently seen in menopause.

the woman lying on the exam table, vulnerable
stripped bare
only hears

*INADEQUATE*
*INCOMPETENT*
*ELDERLY*
*SENILE*

Ashamed.

# What the Old Guys are Telling Us About Us

*1970 onward*

*Everywhere*

the female body as historical text.

hymen:
> from the Greek, virginal membrane
> same word as the Greek god of marriage

nymphae:
> (old word for labia minora or small vaginal lips)
> from the Greek and Latin, bride or beautiful young maiden

vagina:
> from the Latin, sheath, scabbard, or close covering
> in other words—something to stick a penis into

uterus:
> from the Latin, womb, belly
> from the Greek hystera, womb

Fallopian tube:
> named after a sixteenth century Italian Catholic
> priest and anatomist
> Gabriel Fallopius
> (who apparently liked to dissect dead women)

ovary:
> from the Latin, egg, possibly bird

it seems our body parts
are mostly named for what men can do with them using their

penis:
> from the Latin, tail.

# Why We Have a Clitoris

*1970 onward*

*Everywhere*

mid-1600s
Regnier de Graff
Dutch physician and anatomist
described the development of
the ovarian follicle (home of our precious eggs)
now called the Graafian follicle.
(figures it's named after a man)

discovered an erogenous zone in the vagina
later named the Grafenberg Spot or G Spot.

wrote of the clitoris:

> *If these parts of the pudendum*
> *had not been endowed with such*
> *an exquisite sensitivity to pleasure*
> *no woman would be willing*
> *to take upon herself*
> *the irksome nine-months-long business*
> *of gestation*
> *the painful and often fatal process*
> *of expelling the fetus*
> *the worrisome and care-ridden task*
> *of raising children.*

here's what I think he thought:

women just having pleasure
SHOCKING!
for the sake of pure pleasure
SCANDALOUS!
alone or together
HERESY!
they might as well be

MEN.

# Freudian Slips in Two Parts

*1971 to 1972*

*Boston University School of Medicine*

*Boston, Massachusetts*

## On Psychiatry

when I was six
I announced I was going to be
a psychiatrist.
(have twelve children AND
twenty-four animals)

how did I even know that big word?
maybe I liked the way it felt
bouncing on my tongue
how the grownups all smiled
clucking approvingly.
(such a precocious child)

I wrote a paper on schizophrenia in ninth grade
organized a hair salon
at Massachusetts Mental Hospital in twelfth.
(even psychotically depressed women
want to look their best
for their therapists)

they shared their murkiest secrets
with me
as I suds, rinsed
primped, sprayed
listening intently.

I majored in psychology at Bryn Mawr College
running rats, pigeons, cats
through a variety of experiments
implanted electrodes and cannula in their brains
waded through Freud, Jung
Personality Theory.

medical school changed all that.
starting with the psychiatry textbook:

Theodore Lidz, *The Person: His* [sic] *Development throughout the
Life Cycle*, 1968, 558 pages.

pages 369 to 384: Occupational Choice
(regarding men only)

pages 383 to 384: Occupational Choice for Women.
I quote (in verse):

> "Problems of vocational choice are
> more significant to men
> than to women, for whom, by and large,
> marriage and child rearing
> take precedence over career.
> The future of most women depends
> to a frightening degree
> upon whom they marry. . . ."

> "The young woman is very likely
> to choose an occupation in which
> she fills a helping, ancillary position
> or a more or less maternal role."

> **"Women do not usually need to prove themselves
> through accomplishment and achievement,
> gain more satisfaction from being
> admired and loved
> because of who they are,
> or because of what they can give . . ."**

[bolding is my outrage]

> "For with the vast majority of women
> **the choice of occupation is less critical
> than the choice of a husband."**

silently fury.

the analyst who pointed us out from our classmates and announced
(disapprovingly)

*You women are taking the place of a productive male.*

the psychiatrist who looked out at the few women
scattered in the hall

>*You are here because of your Unresolved Penis Envy.*

we medical students
striving
    smart
        determined
            bossy
                angry
women

obviously
deviants.

## Oh, That Fucking Textbook

Dr. Lidz

Professor and Chairman

Department of Psychiatry

Yale University School of Medicine.

A Very Respected and Influential Man.

may I call you Theodore?

I'm not quite done with you.

you wrote:
"pregnancy-related nausea and vomiting
resolves"
page 94

"If the woman is mature and happily married"
[data-free assumption]

"[Then] the pregnancy . . . turns
into a period of blooming
when she experiences
a sense of completion
and self-satisfaction.
**If the mother has come to terms
with being a woman,
which includes some
lingering regrets
at not having been born a
boy . . ."**

**[really Freud]**

"she feels that her pregnancy
is fulfilling her fate,
completing her life as a woman,
and she knows a creativity
that compensates
for past restrictions
and limitations."

[woman as empty vessel yearning to be filled
by a baby
a penis
an analyst's fantasies]

you wrote:
"The adolescent girl"
page 309

**"may still resent the boy's greater freedom**
to explore his world,
and the societal expectations
that she grow up **to be**
**a housekeeper and**
**nursemaid."**

[is that how you see your mother?]

"Still serious resentments usually derive
from **a feeling**
**that anyone without a penis**
**is a cipher."**

[Merriam Webster dictionary:
cipher: pronounced "si" as in "eye"—"fer"
*One that has no weight, worth, or influence:*
*NONENTITY*]

you continued:

"Though such potential dissatisfactions
with being female may exist,
they are usually overshadowed
by the adolescent's pride
in her new status
as a woman,
the acquisition of a physique
that attracts attention,
and the value of the capacity
to bear children.
**If she does not possess a penis,**
**she can have an attractive body**
which she begins to groom
with an unconscious

compensatory narcissism. . . .
**although probably every girl
has some regrets
over being female . . .**
most will recognize
some of the advantages
and gain contentment
through building upon these
potential assets."

what can I say?

on parenthood:
page 446

"The wife may fill male roles
while the husband cooks
and cares for the house.
**But a father cannot properly
"mother' the child . . .
the gender difference
between the parents
properly designates and provides
different tasks for each."**

[translation: men can't rock a crying baby
sing a child to bed
kiss a booboo,
because of their penis?XO!]

on middle age
pages 462 to 463

"In general, middle age is a more critical
and difficult period for [women].
The end of the children's dependency . . .
affects a mother more . . ."

"The middle-aged woman . . .
is still young enough
to start on a new career,
re-enter an old one,
or devote herself more fully

to some activity
she had pursued part-time
while occupied with her children . . ."

"The woman's life will change again
when her husband retires
and their days can be spent together
**and he wishes to have
her companionship."**

[since her job, dreams, aspirations have no value, right?]

on menopause:
pages 464 to 465

"The folklore handed down among women
[about menopause]
engenders the belief that
the menopause causes
serious emotional
and mental instability,
and that a woman is fortunate
if she does not
become seriously depressed
or insane.
The physical symptoms are amplified
into an almost unbearable suffering,
**another burden to which
the deprived sex is subjected."**

[I'm literally tearing my hair out]

"A relationship exists between
the difficulties experienced
during menstrual periods,
childbirth,
and the menopause;
**They are difficulties that relate to
attitudes toward womanhood."**

[ALERT: this statement is devoid
of any scientific basis]

"She knows [with menopause and aging]
She will lose more than her menses
and fertility:
her breasts will grow flabby,
the subcutaneous adipose tissue
that softens her contours
gradually disappears,
her skin becomes wrinkled and sags,
and pouches appear under her eyes.
**Ultimately she will again assume
a rather sexless appearance . . ."**

[are you fucking kidding me?
you treat female patients????]

like a salmon dying
after spawning, I presume.

there is no description of the aging man
presumably he and his penis remain
eternally attractive.

by the end of the course
I was heading towards
a more radical politics
in the midst of my own midlife crisis
looking
for a new career.

# Dangerous Women

*1973*

*Winchester Hospital*

*Winchester, Massachusetts*

I insisted on supporting the woman
almost sitting up
pulling her legs back with each contraction.

we called that a *semi-squat.*

> *no flat on your back*
> *legs in stirrups*
> *anti-gravity position invented by the womanizing Louis XIV*
> *so he could watch his wives and mistresses give birth.*

the head of the obstetrics department took me aside
for a scolding.

he explained:

> *The perineum* (i.e., the area around the vagina)
> *is dangerous for the newborn head.*
> *There is a sudden change in pressure*
> *as the head emerges from that tight place*
> *into the wide wide world.*
> *To protect the baby it is important to make*
> *a big episiotomy* (cut open the vagina*)*
> *apply* (hard metal) *forceps around the baby's head*
> *lift* (pull) *the baby out safely, slowly*
> *in a controlled fashion*
> *from the* (extremely dangerous) *mother.*

I was

> *(extremely)*
>             unconvinced.

## The Paleolithic Era

*1973*

*Boston University School of Medicine*

*Brockton, Massachusetts*

I took my general surgery rotation
at Brockton Hospital
in the Paleolithic Era
or thereabouts.

my shoulders ached from hours of holding retractors.

> *Lift the liver, just a bit higher dear, good, a bit more.*

I rarely could see
what was actually going on down there
the roiling bowels, glistening gall bladders, flaming appendices.

I drank gallons of coffee to stay awake
crumpling into an open abdomen
was frowned upon
and would ruin my grade.

but I did learn some unexpected lessons.

surgeon A drove up in his shiny yellow Cadillac
with the wide sneering grill
fancy tailfins
driving me to his office from the hospital
broad-faced, shiny forehead
self-satisfied bulging gut.
(I wondered about *his* liver)

when I opened the car door
he looked me up and down
frowned at my neatly pleated pants
and said

> *I don't let my women dress like that.*

I worried about *his women,*
his wife, daughters, mistresses, secretaries, office nurses, OR nurses . . .
and now, it seems

me.

surgeon B had a shock of brown hair
a young man's body
he was given to temper tantrums in the operating room
humiliating his faithful scrub nurse
yelling at orderlies and medical students.

when he was really enraged
he threw scalpels.

after finishing a case
he retreated to
the men's change room.

to discuss the operation
the disease process
the prognosis
with other students and colleagues.

leaving me pressed against the door
uninvited
straining to hear.

surgeon C
asked me to join him
at a patient's bedside
a hospital administrator walked in
stared and said.

> *What are you? Housekeeping?*

surgeon C said nothing.

doctors were not supposed
to look like
me.

## Career Choice

*1972 to 1974*

*Boston University School of Medicine*

*Boston, Massachusetts*

the guiding star of psychiatry
faded into the black hole
of arrogance and sexism.

what was I going to be?

on my pediatrics rotation
I imagined a life of sore throats and runny noses
tiny koala bears dangling from my stethoscope
a puppet in my pocket
Mickey Mouse and Daffy Duck
staring me down from cheerful exam room walls
angst-filled teenagers
grappling with desire, STDs, and unplanned
pregnancies.

women were encouraged to do that.
(we're a natural with kids, right?)

anesthesiology?
the hours were good
the people were nice.
the patients, mostly asleep.

internal medicine?
elderly folks
with high blood pressure, diabetes, obesity, cancer
bodies less cooperative
less likely to heal
old cars coming in for tune ups
tire changes
new batteries.

should I specialize?

cardiology?
thumping, swooshing heart sounds
stethoscopes pressed to chests
pouring over EKGs
thin spaghetti lines
to be deciphered
verdicts rendered
procedures ordered
drugs prescribed.

I watched my classmates
find mentors
fall in love with a field
an organ
a path
a life.

I asked myself
as a FEMINIST AND A WOMAN

where would I make
The Most Impact?

not the usual question.

The answer
as a FEMINIST AND A WOMAN
was Painfully Obvious.

the field that felt most Backward
Most Important for Women
Most In Need of Big Time Radical Surgery
at the hands of an angry, ambitious lady doctor.

Obstetrics and Gynecology.

I debated
struggled with my sisters
circles of consciousness raising late into the night.

could I survive five years of training?
years of surgical instruction?
attitudes that made me crazy?

no mentor?
a life of disrupted nights?

hours treating routine birth control
       vaginal infections
              menopausal hot flashes
interrupted by life-threatening
       ruptured ectopic pregnancies and mad rushes
           to the operating room?

could I give my life to that?

perhaps in honor of the brother I couldn't save
when I was three.

       close that primal wound
       devote myself to women
       filled with babies
       who needed to be safely accompanied
       into this world.

that is where I wanted to be.

for all those reasons.

I packed my dynamite
filled out my applications.

readied for battle.

# Trust

*Early 1970s*

*Brookline, Massachusetts*

he was hip, young
I could trust him
he listened.

most of the female medical students
went to his office
for birth control and other gynecologic woes
getting pregnant was so out of the question
at this moment in our lives.

he said the Dalkon Shield IUD
        was the newest best thing in contraception
           after insertion
              no worries.

in 1971 the Dalkon Shield was
the hottest contraceptive on the market.

                within a few years
                researchers noted
                pelvic infections
           infected unintended pregnancies
                infertility
           young women dying.

by 1974 the IUD was
off the market

          but the devices already inserted
              were not recalled
              until 1984
         after thousands of lawsuits
       millions of dollars in compensation
            punitive damages.

the drug company filed for bankruptcy
in 1985.

        the IUD was not rigorously tested
      by the US Food and Drug Administration

because it was not a drug.

but I couldn't know this yet.

every month, when the roiling cramps began
I found myself in a puddle of blood
(in the middle of a lecture or other awkward moment)
I swore I would tell him to take it out
every month the storm passed.

I was so busy
it was so easy
it was so reliable

*I'll see if it gets better.*

it didn't.

after one night rocking in pain and fever
the phone call
pelvic inflammatory disease
antibiotics.
I finally had enough.

he took it out.

he was so understanding.
he fitted me with a trusty
old fashioned diaphragm.

maybe he was the kind of doctor
I wanted to be.

months later
he was accused of
fondling a mother's breasts
and other parts
as she dozed in the hospital
exhausted from baby birthing.

did the nurse walk
into the darkened room
find him
touching an intimate part
of the woman's body?

did the mother startle awake
when her infant cried
to discover her doctor
in her bed
in some passionate embrace
with her exhausted breasts?

he defended himself saying
something about how
birth is love
oneness and beauty
merging together
in this magical moment
that he was part of.

right.

he lost his license.
moved to Florida.
sold real estate.

another powerful man assaulting vulnerable women.

I vowed to stick with
women doctors.

no guarantees
but I needed to up the odds.

# Physical Exam

*1972*

*Boston University School of Medicine*

*Boston, Massachusetts*

male students
stripped to the waist
breaking the boundaries between
social touch and medical touch.

> (usually, students do not take their clothes off
> during class
> usually, we do not touch each other's naked bodies
> in class, anyway)

chests smooth, pale, freckled, skinny, bulgy, bearlike
nervous laughter
I tentatively applied my shiny, cold stethoscope
feeling all serious and professional
listened carefully for the thump-thump, thump-thump
not sure where to put my other hand
hunted for murmurs, arrhythmias

> *take a deep breath.*

the whooshing air sounds
my newfound foreign language
wheezes
     crackles
          stridor
               rhonchi
                    rales.

a secret code
the first steps into
THE CLUB.

they wouldn't let the women
strip

because of
you know
OUR BREASTS.

the class learned *that* on a plastic
not-at-all-like-the-real-thing model
we called Betty the Boob.

the abdomen was easier
we unzipped our pants
stretched out on the tables
scooted down the undies
(not too far)
cool unsure hands pressed
into soft gut, feeling for liver edge
masses hidden in doughy flesh.

I practiced testing cranial nerves with a routine:
stick tongue out
      clench teeth
           squeeze eyes shut
                follow the light
                    shrug shoulders
                        nod when the vibrations
                            from the tuning fork
                              are audible.

audible, arrhythmia, auscultation
a magical language leading me toward doctorhood.

the pelvic exam was a frightful combination of
dismay, discomfort, curiosity
the *models?*

prostitutes.

      (who else would be willing to have
      a clutch of shaky, sweaty gloved hands
      poke and prod that private place
      again and again
      for a price?)

the woman spread her legs
silently
an anonymous crotch.

that did not feel right.

I wanted to say
to all the men in my class
(but didn't)

> *this woman is a person.*
>
> *when you do a pelvic exam*
> *imagine yourself*
> *buck naked*
> *legs in cold metal stirrups*
> *your jewels hanging limply in the cool office air*
> *a gloved hand poking and prodding*
> *squeezing your balls*
> *judging*
> *telling you to breathe normally.*
>
> *just imagine that.*

we never practiced
the rectal exam
on men.

I guess, no volunteers
or the price was too high.

spiffed and buffed in a starched white coat
my name pinned to my front pocket
(real doctor-like)
a respectable dress, sensible shoes
wild hair corralled in a bun
my face framed by the most demure
of my hippie earrings
I drove to Chelsea Naval Hospital
to see my first *practice patient*
the institution—all male docs

        male nurses
                male patients
and me.

I spent hours writing out
all my history and physical exam questions
on white file cards
a clipboard ready
to record
THE ANSWERS.

cloaked in nervous anticipation
stethoscope casually draped around my neck
clutching a shiny, black pretend-alligator skin
doctor's bag, gift from a pharmaceutical company
I arrived at the nurses' station
took the card with my patient's name
sailed down the open ward
as if I had done this a thousand times before.

I pulled the curtain around my assignment:
an unconscious, jaundiced male with skinny legs and a massive belly.

overwhelming relief!
I knew his diagnosis: hepatic encephalopathy.

        translation: severe -probably alcoholic- cirrhosis of the liver
        leading to a deluge of toxins
        that affected his brain.

        translation: I didn't have to talk with him.

I leaned my file cards up against his still body
tenting the sheets
started my exam
beginning at the top of his pale, yellowed head.

my second *practice patient*
was a strapping, muscular, crew-cut
Navy man
probably my age
I had my shield of file cards and clipboard

and was doing a respectable job of
appearing to be a thorough, unusually obsessive doctor.

until I got to the hernia exam.

I hadn't quite figured out the technicalities of that.

how to reach down and stick my finger into
the sides of his testicles.

do I face him?
stand behind him?
lift up the gown?

somehow in my flurry of incompetence
I ended up on my knees facing him.

he was stark naked.

when I asked him to cough
his penis bounced in my face.

I wasn't sure which one of us
was going to die
first.

# Lincoln Hospital Trilogy

## The Very Radical Boyfriend

*1970 to 1975*

*Boston, Massachusetts & New York City, New York*

I met my Very Radical Boyfriend
at a Student Health Organization meeting
weeks after medical school began
moved in with him shortly thereafter.

my parents were not pleased.

he was one year ahead of me
filled with the focused outrage and bravado
that comes with growing up the privileged son of a doctor
during the time of the Vietnam War
feminists fighting the patriarchy
smashing monogamy
Black Panthers organizing free breakfast programs
the assassination of Martin Luther King
police tear gassing and beating anti-war protestors in Chicago
at the 1968 Democratic National Convention
and much, much more.

the Very Radical Boyfriend taunted police
with their snarling German shepherds
at anti-war protests.

ran endless meetings.
(where I sometimes fell asleep, exhausted, overwhelmed, invisible)

he dreamed up Street Theater challenging sexism in the hospital
exposing the doctor as king/the nurse as handmaiden.

I still remember a nurse explaining to me
to be a professional

> *you wear your cap with pride*

the crisp white cap denoting education and rank
tidy hair and modest appearance.

his mind-altering course at Harvard College
on health politics
altered my mind as well.

at night we smoked hash and studied biochemistry
pharmacology, physical diagnosis.

I stopped shaving my legs in an act of protest
against everything that was expected of women.
      (thin, air-brushed, perky, but not-too-troublesome)

wandered through my contradictions
at weekly women's consciousness-raising sessions
unearthing my voice
my fears
my strength.

I wanted to know what he knew.
I wanted some of his bravery.
      (I was the quiet girlfriend
      in the background
      needing to please)

I followed him to the South Bronx
to train at Lincoln Hospital.

got more than I expected.

Lincoln Hospital was limping along.

first built as a home for aging Blacks and former slaves
141st St, just off the six-lane Bruckner Expressway
in the industrial slum called Mott Haven
between crumbling brownstones, a bread factory
the terminal for the Yellow Cab Company.

bathed in the honk and hustle of the inner city
low-flying jets rumbled overhead
on their approach to La Guardia Airport
mingled with the screams of ambulances.

the neighborhood teemed with African Americans
former sharecroppers
    office workers
      typists
        tradesmen
fleeing cotton, tobacco, rice plantations
"colored" schools and lynchings
the *Strange Fruit* of Jim Crow.

heading north after World War I
accelerating into the 1970s.
(The Great Migration)

Puerto Ricans escaping
island poverty and joblessness
collided with Jewish and Irish immigrants
in the tenements of the South Bronx
rapidly turning neighborhoods Black and Brown.
(The Great White Flight)

Lincoln Hospital weathered the transmigrations
a poor orphaned sister in the public hospital system
sinking into a ragged skeleton
of an inner-city teaching hospital
antiquated and overlooked.

like a (so-called) third-world outpost
just east of glittering Manhattan.

## To Be of Use

*1973 to 1975*

*Bronx, New York*

Lincoln Hospital survived
as a last stop before death
resuscitated by an
affiliation with Einstein College of Medicine
where house staff trained on the poor
dreamt of moving on to care for real patients
          (paying, middle class, white)
in private offices
in the cities and suburbs.

as the hospital sank into negligent obscurity
the interns and residents trended brown
increasingly from the
          Philippines
                    India
                              Pakistan
                                        Taiwan.

decent, hardworking Foreign Medical Graduates
unacculturated to
the wants and needs of the American south gone north
and island people surviving the streets of New York.

taken down by alcoholism
heroin addiction
the spilling of blood
by well-armed gangs
police aggression
pulled in disparate directions by church leaders
          pimps
                    local bosses
                              the Black Panthers and Young Lords.

there were angry takeovers
demands for a People's Program

---

a community-run methadone treatment
with a good dose of anticolonial
anti-capitalist political education
and acupuncture.

there were upheavals, sit-ins, arrests
a painted bed sheet flapping from the sixth floor
hanging over the Expressway:
SEIZE THE HOSPITAL TO SERVE THE PEOPLE!

a call went out for house staff
with a *socially and politically conscious orientation*
to come train in the service of the community
to challenge hierarchy and authority
old ways of thinking.

the Collective formed: doctors, nurses, mental health workers
Young Lords with berets and power handshakes
in a heady, messy, uneasy, fractious coalition
ready to make revolution
full of idealism
burdened by a 100-hour work week
and very sick patients.

I wanted to be there.

I wanted to be useful
on the frontlines
in the grit
of medicine and poverty
working for the neglected and forgotten
a transformative challenge to the past.

the boyfriend and I
set up housekeeping
in a cozy place on City Island
the eastern edge of the Bronx
where no one locked their doors
and no one rented to Blacks.

the bay lapped at our dead-end street
tourists lined the one main avenue
looking for good seafood

fried clams, French fries
car radios jangled Puerto Rican salsa.

a pastel mirage of beach, water, land and sky shimmered at sunset.

the daily drive to the South Bronx
was a down-the-rabbit-hole kind of experience
a going to combat
purposeful
overwhelming
fierce.

DC current pulsed through the old Nurses' Residence
patients slept in forty-bed wards
with beds often lined down the center
cardiac monitors chirped
the stink of toilets overflowing
the fetid odors of the unwashed
gangrenous legs twitching with maggots
a shortage of clean linens.

one eight-bed ICU for all comers.

the newly painted pediatric department
poisonous lead paint in its walls.

post call
my roommate would collapse asleep
on the living room rug
too exhausted to climb up to his second floor bedroom
we stepped around him like a piece of furniture
played music, cooked brown rice, veggies, hash brownies
laughed loudly, got stoned.

driving home one evening
bone-weary
I stepped on the gas when everyone stopped.

miraculously
I only crunched my fender

once.

I called all of this
home.

## Lessons from a Fish

*1973 to 1975*

*Bronx, New York*

I heard the call
(and the pull of the Very Radical Boyfriend)
arriving for medical school rotations
and a year-long medical internship.

the Collective was committed to the very good idea that:
      the people served should have a say
      in the policies and direction of an institution
      that (theoretically) served them.

this is way harder than it sounds.

we challenged individualism and arrogance
but were still male-dominated
we engaged in criticism and self-criticism
read quotations from Chairman Mao's Little Red Book
we docs confronted our elitism, our whiteness
but we were all mostly passing through
though our lives and commitment
to the poor, the forgotten, the disenfranchised
were forever changed.

we never built a permanent political coalition
with "The Community"
(which was disorganized, diverse, multi-lingual, and wrestling for
    survival)
we couldn't impact the larger forces
that were crushing the have-nots in our care.

we joined a strike with Montefiore Hospital
for an 80-hour work week
the march led by a young, red-headed doctor whose grandfather
working in the garment industry
had gone on strike years earlier
demanding 40 hours max.

*New York Post:*
March 18, 1975,
3,000 DOCS OUT AT 22 HOSPITALS.

inspired and intimidated
fearful of my walk from the parking lot to the hospital
I felt embraced by the many Black and often gay nurses
and the people who came to my clinics.

I studied the impact of The Community Medical Corps
where health workers went door-to-door
(like barefoot doctors in China)
testing for rampant lead poisoning
      high blood pressure
            tuberculosis.

I learned that many of my patients
wanted me to wear a white coat
as a symbol of respect, not privilege.

the small rectangular on-call room in the old Nurses' Residence
two single beds, a light bulb hanging from the ceiling (prison-like)
the ancient shared bathroom
with its cracked tile and crumbling plaster
moldy smell
the shower with a single sad jet of water
cockroaches scattering when I switched the light
got even more creepy
when the head of the methadone detoxification clinic was found
crumpled in one of the underground tunnels
that connected the hospital buildings
perhaps murdered by a drug-pusher
overdosed with a fatal hit of heroin.

after that
if there ever was a lull in my nights on call
I slept on the patients' floor
dozing on a hard exam table.

I learned to draw blood from an addict's foot
(when all other veins were scarred)
to pour ice water into the lavage

when a young, alcoholic man
arrived vomiting bright red blood from enormous ruptured varicose
    veins
in his esophagus
(cirrhosis of the liver)
while his wife and mother keened and wept
washing his body with Spanish prayers and sorrows
love and grief.

I learned to run to the ICU when the electricity failed
attach bags to ventilators and pump life-giving breaths into
two patients side-by-side
the back-up generators didn't always work.

sometimes we ran out of penicillin
IV tubing.
(in New York City, America in the Twentieth Century)

I held the spidery hands
of a young Black man in sickle cell crisis
sobbing in pain
as morphine dripped into his battered veins.

road ambulances
at night
boxy vehicles with poor suspension
the city's lights flashed across my face
while patients writhed in agony
squeezed my hand, crying

               *Doctora, doctora.*

Lincoln was often at full capacity
we disgorged anyone who could survive the transfer.

I watched in horror after a gang shoot-out on the hospital emergency
    ramp
we dragged in bodies like a scene from Vietnam
or police delivering a dead gang member
one of them sporting the ear he had sliced off as a trophy.

I took amphetamines and mainlined coffee (virtually)
to stay awake the last 12 hours

of my 36 hour shifts
smoked weed to lull myself into restless, broken sleep
lived on starchy hospital food
plantains, rice and beans, spicy chicken
from the local taqueria.

I chuckled at the irony that
I (a female doctor who was supposed to be male)
had to catheterize the male patients
the old guys grinning and making raucous jokes
as I reached for their lonely, limp penises.

but mostly, I loved my patients.
the elderly Black woman who confused
a tiny Asian-faced Filipina intern
with me, Eastern European, easily twice her size.

> *You both have the same smile*, she grinned.

I met the battered poor, tricking death over and over
inviting me and my colleagues to join in battle.
a full-blown case of Cushing's Disease
totally out of control diabetes
the ravages of addiction
each patient a blur of
       fluids
           testing
               electrolytes
                  chemistries,
                      electrocardiograms
the terror of the moment neatly compartmentalized
for maximum functionality
rule number one
for survival.

there was no preventive care
no elective admissions
old charts were stored topsy turvy
in a huge upstairs room, water-damaged.

I took to carrying a growing stack of file cards listing
every patient I cared for

their problem list and medications
bulging in my pocket.

but mostly I learned a lot of medicine
from folks who were willing to teach me
about their symptoms and findings
persistence and dignity
survival in a place with little forgiveness.

I learned to be humble and respectful.

I remember an older African American man
with severe high blood pressure
arrived faithfully at my clinic
with a large fish wrapped in newspaper
proudly stretched out his hands.

> *I caught this for you, doc.*

I shook my head no
how could I accept this gift
from a destitute person living on the edge of hunger?

humiliated, he stood up
took his fish
and walked out.

## *For the times they are a-changin'*
## Bobby Zimmerman aka Bob Dylan

*1971 to 1982*

*Boston, Massachusetts*

my medical student boyfriend and I
liked the idea of group living
less lonely—one of us was always
studying
working
sleeping
plus we were young and hopeful
filled with disdain for old ways of doing things.

we got together some medical and graduate students
teachers
   nurses
     writers
       a union organizer
         movement lawyer
           various stragglers
yearning to create a new model
a chosen clan
thoughtful, egalitarian
with the loftier goals of
   reordering the nuclear family
     questioning gender-defined roles
       redistributing the wealth
        having a good time
it was a long and hefty list.

I cashed in some New England Nuclear stock
the boyfriend sold his Bar Mitzvah Bonds for Israel
we had $9,000 for the down payment
on a roomy two-family
in the Allston neighborhood of Boston
it was a lot of house and yard for $32,900
the mortgage, $198 a month.

                                   St Anthony's Parish, Boston Irish
                                    embraced by the old stone church
                                               and Catholic school
                                      where everyone feared the nuns
                                                 minded the priests
                                                 and the old ladies
                              played bingo in the church basement
                                                   Thursday night.

the U-Haul trucks pulled away
slowly moving down Aldie Street
blocks of two to three-story wooden houses
firefighters, police men
construction workers, teachers
college students, stay-at-home moms
tucked between the
          Mass Pike
          Charles River
          ever encroaching
          Harvard University.

we lugged in our boxes, bed-frames, lamps
up the front stairs, across the porch
gashed the wall of the stairwell
as we shimmied the fridge
up to the second floor kitchen
divided the twelve rooms
into eight bedrooms
          dining room
                    common space
filled with sunshine and aspiring (unrealistic) dreams.

Sunday mornings
we watched the (relatively) faithful
parade down to church
seeking neighborly camaraderie
comfort in the Father, Son, and Holy Ghost.

we negotiated our new home
held endless meetings to discuss and debate

cooking
chores
shopping
gardening
interviewing new members
disappointments
> (don't leave the kitchen a mess, take the trash out
> > on time, clean the bathroom
> blah blah blah
> the boring stuff that gets very important)

rent was according to income
every month's rent gave a member part-ownership in the house
food costs were split equally
nothing was ever written down because

we trusted each other.

> neighborhood boys
> egged our bay windows.

> *Dirty hippies.*
> *Bearded long-haired*
> *(unmarried) men*
> *and (unshaven) women*
> *living together.*
> *Bring down the*
> *housing prices*
> *for sure.*

there were rumors of an anti-Black gang
our friends were vigilant.

we joined the local food co-op
lugged cardboard boxes
freighted with fruits and veggies
fresh eggs
brown rice.

shopped in bulk at Haymarket Square
a big open expanse of outdoor stalls and pushcarts
in the North End, the old Italian section

rough and tumble vendors hawking
great assortments of cheese and prosciutto
lamb chops, forty cents a pound
towers of tomatoes, squash
the empty boxes and rotting vegetables
tossed into the street.

I set up a potter's wheel and kiln in the basement
the cool wet clay
a soothing balm in my hands
shelves against the rough foundation
with rows of rounded bowls and mugs
waiting to be fired.

there were nightly dinners
with a tendency towards whole grains
extravagant desserts
good times
great parties
a bountiful vegetable garden
a team to shovel the snow
dig out the cars
pull the trash can into the cleared spot
marking the space as TAKEN.

always someone for a talk
or a hallucinatory smoke.

when one waif-like woman
plunged into insanity, cut her wrists
needed hospitalization
schizophrenia
we coaxed her into treatment
put her on a plane
sent her home to her parents.

a good supportive community.

until it was not.

we were too optimistic.

I missed much of the joy, the drama
relationships made and undone
I was always
studying
working
sleeping
bouncing between training in
Boston and New York.

my love life imploded.

I ate too much chocolate and peanut butter crackers
drank too much coffee
stayed awake jazzed and caffeinated
all night
delivering babies.

started jogging by the river
described myself in a tumultuous journal as
*Dr. Detached in Perpetual Loneliness.*

a poster in my room read:
*A woman without a man is like a fish without a bicycle.*

I fantasized announcing to the house
*I am now a boarder—will not share cooking, burdens, etc.*
*I get so little in return.*

I took care of women in the neighborhood
knew about their troubled marriages
            unplanned pregnancies
                    abortions
slapped a prochoice sticker on my orange VW Rabbit
relieved my tires weren't slashed.

house members changed
moved on
shifted allegiances
didn't grow up
resentments sprouted
there was less cooperation
more grownup adults living cheaply
easily

in a nice big house I was mostly
paying for.

eleven years later
after an ugly battle
with the folks still there
over mundane matters like
money
politics
obligation.

I paid out all their shares
moved back in
newly married.

they left the place
a mess.

resentment will do that.

the times hadn't changed
quite enough.

# The Haircut

*1973*

*Boston, Massachusetts*

when I was young
my father
would sit my little brother
in a chair outside
      cut his
      thick curly hair
until one day
      he nipped off the tip of his
      ear.

as I got older
I often wondered if that was some
subconscious Abraham-struggling-with-god-over-Isaac
kind of moment.

      just a little snip.

in any case
at twelve
I got the family
barbershop job.

my brother was my only client.

in my mid-twenties
my dearest friend and housemate
had a waist-length mane of
thick straight black-as-night hair.

she wanted a new do.

      *Sure* I said
      chutzpah being my middle name.

we locked the bathroom door
she stripped to her underwear
stood in front of the sink.

I made a braid almost the size
of my arm
tied both ends with a rubber band
took the scissors.

CHOP.

>my stomach churned
>*Oh god what have I done?*

fear and daring got to work
snipping, shaping
short rounded in the back
>curving towards her neck
>>longer tapered in the front
>>>cupping her face

actually
quite lovely.

she turned around
leaned on the sink
to admire her reflection
in the opposite mirror.

a sudden grinding sound
the ancient pipe below the sink
fractured
spilling a jet of water
onto the tile floor
fire hosing her bottom.

as the bathroom flooded
she screamed

>*DON'T COME IN!*

Being Very Shy
even in times of emergency.

I threw her a towel
got the door open
as she frantically held up the sink.

house mates mobilized
raced down the cellar
eyes on the ceiling
tracing the maze of geriatric pipes
located the turn off.

relief.

the tallest guy wrenched it closed.

the segment of pipe fractured
fell into his hand
raining water on his head.

we were laughing and screaming so hard
it was almost impossible
to rise to this new catastrophe.

a scramble of detective work
(what did we know about houses?)
traced the pipes down to the
the main house shut off.

          I felt I worked in an old tradition
          the first barbers
          were also surgeons
          this was part of my destiny.

              maybe
              I should have been
              a plumber.

# Ni hao ma?

1973

People's Republic of China

a grey bird
fluttered through the open window
of the operating room
as a middle-aged patient
lay comfortably
on the OR table
eating sliced pears
chatting through the interpreter.

the surgeon
leaned over the pear eater
took scalpel to
    skin
    subcutaneous fat
    fascia
    pleura
resecting
a piece of lung
while the acupuncturist poked
tweaking the needles
like skinny porcupine quills
jabbed into the body.

    my astonishment crashed into disbelief
    which lapsed into humility
    how could this be?
    acupuncture?
    no other anesthesia?
    impossible!

I was in medical school
on a student tour of China
shortly after the fiercely anti-communist
President Nixon
chatted up Mao Zedong

toured the Great Wall
mixed dumplings
with diplomacy
beginning the unlikely "thaw"
between these two countries.

here I was
taking it all in
a grand, discombobulating adventure.

the next person
was having a thyroid nodule removed
the surgeon explained
　　　　　through the interpreter
that he appreciated an awake and chattering patient
so he could avoid damaging the nerve
to the vocal cord.

the patient
　　　　　through the interpreter
welcomed us to China
sending greetings and friendship
to the people of America.

　　　　　　　　　　an extraordinary clash
　　　　　　between my understanding of
　　　　　　　　　　Western healthcare
　　　　　　　　　how the body worked
　　　　　　　　　what was possible
　　　　　　and this 5,000-year-old
　　　　　　　　　system of medicine.

did I mention this was humbling?
changed my attitudes for life?
blew open my preconceptions
of just about everything?

everywhere we toured
from factories to schools
to peasant villages
wrinkled women

*spoke bitterness*
emptying the hunger and suffering
of their lives
into our laps
extolling the new China
      food
             housing
                    possibility.

it was the end of the Cultural Revolution
an uprising of the workers against their bosses
students in the vanguard
a great re-equilibration
purging capitalists and reactionary thinkers.

seemed like a pretty good idea at the time.

      (it wasn't.
      Mao was consolidating his fanatical power
        with re-education camps
      ruined lives
      hundreds of thousands
      maybe millions massacred
      humiliated
      tortured.)

we didn't know.

we met ordinary people
who were no longer hungry
who had jobs and hope
housing and healthcare.

everywhere we traveled
traffic jams of bicyclists
young and old
collided
staring at us
as if we were space invaders
an open, heart-felt curiosity.

one student asked me

>    *Are you Japanese?*

he knew *they* were foreigners
so why not?

it was a good guess.

at night when we traveled by bus
the driver flicked the headlights on and off
mostly off
(I assume to save the light bulb)
honking, as the wave of bicyclists parted
like the Red Sea
flashes of blue/grey Mao jackets
the national uniform
heads bobbing, pigtails flying
black shoes rising and falling
in the intermittent light.

on the last day of the delegation
we chewed and smiled our way
through our final, sumptuous banquet
>        (real Chinese food having nothing to do
>        with chop suey and fried rice)
extended the bonds of friendship
took the last clutch of photos.

one of our guides took me aside
earnestly
looked intently into my eyes
smiled warmly.

>        *As a doctor, you should*
>        *always remember to*
>        *serve the people.*

his words
part advice
part
blessing.

# See No Evil

*1974*

*Brookdale Hospital*

*Brooklyn, New York*

the woman sat up in bed, rocking, groaning
(fathers still not allowed in labor and delivery)
her chestnut hair matted
rubbing her swollen belly
hut-hut-hooing herself to full cervical dilation
bathed in the earthy scents of blood and amniotic fluid.

I was so excited to see a mother
doing natural childbirth
     focused
         breathing
             in touch with the rhythms of labor
                  she had taken all the classes
                       she wanted to have her
                         baby
                         HER WAY.

she was in control in a totally out-of-control moment.

(birthing being wildly primordial)

when she pushed with all her fierceness
I felt the magnificent power of her body
a primal life-giving force, womb-goddess-like
channeling the women
who labored and birthed before her.

I was awestruck.

as the baby's head began to crown
my heart quickened.

but

the anesthesiologist snapped a mask over her face

*Take the edge off, dear.*

her obstetrician whipped out his forceps
cut a huge episiotomy opening her vagina
slipped the forceps over the baby's head
and

           dragged
              it
                  out
                      the
                          last
                              inch
                                  of
                                      the
                                          birth canal.

robbing her.

the doc turned to me
eyes like darts over his mask.

      *he held his hands over his ears* (you didn't hear that)
      *his eyes* (you didn't see that)
      *his mouth (*you will keep silent)
      *his crotch* (you will not say what I did)

Got it?

# Vortex

*1974*

*Spofford Juvenile Detention Center*

*Bronx, New York*

I held the murderer's warm penis
in my gloved hand
a blustery anxious
fifteen-year-old
freakin' that the drip was
*gong-a-rhea*
and some white lady was holding
his manhood with a sterile white swab
in her other white hand.

the only additional murderer
in juvie
was fourteen
pregnant
thrilled she was making
a baby to love
be loved
brewing a future
she never had
      onesies
            formula
                  baby carriage
                        crib
hers.

hundreds of children
slept in decrepit, locked, cellblock-like rooms
barred windows, long dark hallways
open toilets and showers
the building complex encased in rusted concertina wire
like a modern day dystopian
Grimm fairy tale

the rare parent showing up on
visiting day.

kids accused of
       rape

             arson

                  assault

                       armed robbery.

awaited trial or punitive placement elsewhere
in this failed attempt at
juvenile justice.

in the detention clinic
I was a sub-intern
assigned through the Adolescent Medicine Department
Montefiore Hospital
I worked like a doc
my fourth year of med school.
(which is to say, without the MD at the end of my name)

a coveted kind of experience
that was permitted
mostly for doctoring
the have-nots
who had run out of choices
in a system already leaning up against them.

as I treated
       runny noses
          lice
             VD
                 pregnancy.

patched up stab wounds
          broken hearts (delinquents still yearn big, desire
             more, fall in love, crash)
             suicide attempts

my spirit ached
for these battered, damaged, easily triggered
dream-filled brown and black children

angry, giggly, frightened
already caught
in a vortex of destruction
        stabbings
                drug use
                        abuse
                                gangs
                                        callous sex.
at home
on the streets
inside this prison.

locked up
plagued by roaches, rats
grim peeling lead paint.

for some, three meals and four cigarettes a day
bedtime snack
a TV in the dayroom
was a step up
from what they called
home.

I offered
a moment of kindness
judgment-free
in this negligent world
as broken
as they were.

while they hurtled along
on a tortured journey
to nowhere
good.

# Internal Medicine, Final Exam

*1974*

*Boston University School of Medicine*

*Boston, Massachusetts*

curtains drawn
the older man lay in his hospital bed.

he smiled at me.

> *I know this is a final exam, dear.*
> *I want you to do well.*

my swelling anxiety
crashed on the shores of his reassurance.

I took out my pen
my lined pad of paper
my list of questions.

History and Physical Exam.

he walked me through his symptoms
pointed out his arthritic hands
his enormous spleen
with a sparkle in his eyes
he mentioned his low white count.

a wave of relief
nearly knocked me over.

FELTY'S SYNDROME?

I had just done a literature review
on this incredibly rare autoimmune disease
I knew next to nothing about diabetes
high blood pressure.

but Felty's Syndrome?
World Expert.

I left the hospital
with an ebullient sense of victory

and crashed my car
at an intersection on the way back to school.

## The Details

*mid-1950s to 1970s*

*Wherever I was*

phosphorescence
fifth grade science fair
first prize.

remember?

always tried to be your science girl.

you gave me money during
medical school.

　　　　*For tuition and expenses.*

I still remember what you said.

　　　　*I don't approve of your lifestyle.*

(commune? boyfriend? smoking dope? did he even know?)

　　　　*Just don't tell me what you're doing.*

your face at graduation
as they placed that dark hood
over my scarlet academic gown
gold tasseled

　　　　　MEDICAL DOCTOR

you looked like a puffed up
　　　　rooster
　　　　　　strutting
　　　　　　　B-E-A-M-I-N-G.

you loved the idea of me
the physician
with the Harvard appointment.

the details?

not so much.

# Passover—The Order Of Things

*1970s to 1990s*

*Brookline, Massachusetts*

family holidays
that pull of obligation, yearning
infantilization, disappointment
friction.

mom, the ever gracious (anxious) host
in the kitchen for days
getting ready
cleansing the house of *chometz*
bread, pasta, cookies, crackers, pretzels
(leavened foods from grains
deemed unkosher for passover)
like a massive obsessive spring cleaning
for god.

I succumbed to the invitation
part expectation, part demand
a traditional passover seder
the ritual telling of the Jewish exodus from Egypt
a bustle of chopping, roasting, baking
a reading of the haggadah.

the youngest child singing
the four questions
*mah nishtanah halailah hazeh mikol haleilot?*
(why is this night different from all other nights?)

the elders answering them
in song and prayer
with symbolic foods
hard boiled eggs
lamb shanks
bitter herbs
matzah.

a holiday with promising opportunities
to celebrate
struggle
liberation
justice.

I arrived godless
with a phalanx of housemates
armed with my discomfort
on alert
in enemy territory.

my father was about to begin
when my mother interrupted
wanting to say a few words.
(off script)

they verbally scuffled
publicly
(a shocking quarrel
in front of guests and family)

tension exploded in the air
like a deftly thrown hand grenade.

she won.

*passover is one of my*
*favorite holidays*
*because seder means*
*order*
*the father leads the haggadah*
she smiled benevolently
victoriously
*and the children only ask . . .*
*the right questions.*

I cringed
the bitter irony of my
dethroned father
sitting quietly
punctuated by
the not-so-veiled warning
from my mother.

when it came time
to bless and drink the first
of four glasses of wine
*borukh ato adonoy, eloheynu melekh olom*
*borey pri hagofen*
(blessed are you, adonai our god, ruler of the universe
creator of the fruit of the vine)
my Very Radical Boyfriend
pulled out his hash pipe
announced he would take a toke
while we sipped.

it was only fair, his drug of choice
he said.

my mother bristled
horrified
embarrassed
(in front of guests)
sent him to the basement
to smoke
alone.

return shot fired.

we were very unruly
children.

score: mom—one.

decades later
my brother and I
tired of my
Parents' Passovers
the squirming grandchildren
the bored spouses
the incomprehensible irrelevant prayers.

we staged a revolt
demanded a turn
at running the show.

designed a haggadah
part prayers and rituals

part poems, folksongs, liberation politics
part puppets, games for kids.

as we gathered
I sat down at the head of the table
my father moving toward the same chair.

we squabbled
publicly.

I explained
(as if to a child)
I was leading this seder.

(witness the weeks of debate
the revised updated haggadah
the arguments and negotiations)

my father unwilling
to give up
his seat
his power already
drifting
south.

we ended up
squashed slightly sideways
both at the head
of the table
the corners
poking into our bellies -
an uneasy truce.

score: one—for me
sort of.

# PART FOUR: OBSTETRICS AND GYNECOLOGY

In which the battles for my sanity, my babies, and my work are actually fought.

# Obstetrics and Gynecology Residency Interview

*1974*

*Boston Hospital for Women (aka "The Brigham")*

*Boston, Massachusetts*

the conference room
gradually filled
with Very Important, Smart, White Men

interviewing
me.

at one point
a Very Important, Smart, White Man
asked

> *Are you a feminist?*

I knew this was a trick question
unrelated to my future qualifications
as an obstetrician/gynecologist
but clearly related to my acceptability
into their club.

I demurred.

> *It depends on what you mean.*

the Very Important, Smart, White Man got up
put his arm on my shoulder and said

> *Honey, if you don't know by now*
> *I am not going to tell you.*

I stared silently at him, seething and smiling.

I asked

> *What are the weaknesses in this program?*

there was a shaking of heads.
a look of bewilderment.

I held my breath.

waiting.

no one could think of any.

*The strengths?*

the chief of the department smiled warmly.

*WE ARE A GROUP OF BRIGHT YOUNG MEN,*
*READY TO MAKE OUR MARK ON MEDICINE.*

# Modern Delivery

*1975*

*Beth Israel Hospital*

*Boston, Massachusetts*

what I learned the first week
of my residency
on the night obstetrics rotation
8 p.m. to 8 a.m.
six nights a week.

when a woman arrives in labor
get the IV started quickly.
      (translation: labor is a dangerous life-threatening
          unpredictable process
      she could bleed to death, seize, die or otherwise be
          endangered
      we need to be ready for everything and anything always)

order the enema, if she's not in active labor, wink at the nurse, *A
    Triple H.*
      (translation: High, Hot, and a Hell of a Lot—*that'll get
        her going* )

order the poodle prep, a weird shave of the lower half of the pubic
    hair
leaving a tuft at the top—this was supposed to be an improvement
over the old practice of a full shave.
      (translation: pubic hair, ewwww, I'm suturing here!)

when the head is about to crown
but not too soon *because you will tie up the delivery room*
but not too late *because the baby will arrive in the hall*
(with everyone watching and yelling)
rush to the delivery room
get the woman to *scoot over* from her bed
onto a hard narrow delivery table
(which still has leather straps hanging from the sides
remember twilight sleep?)

while the lady is having contractions and an intense impulse to push
and the nurse is urging
*blow blow blow.*

arrange the woman flat on her back, legs dangling in stirrups
a bright surgical light aimed at the area of interest
everyone around her scrubbed, gowned, masked
as if for major heart surgery.
> (translation: the most important thing at this point is
> that the ob can see his sort-of-sterile surgical field
> and do whatever it is he plans to do)

scrub the lady's bottom with betadine and drape with sterile sheets.
> (translation: a woman's vagina and vulva are a dirty
> hairy, dangerous place
> especially for an obstetrician)

cut a generous episiotomy.
> (translation: a woman's vagina and pelvic floor are pressing
> on the vulnerable baby's head
> not built quite right for the job)

it's a miracle anyone survived birth
before we came along
and improved everything.

# The Thing Is

(version published *Mobius, The Journal of Social Change* 2021)

*1975*

*Beth Israel Hospital*

*Boston, Massachusetts*

The thing is

he was a prominent doctor famous man leader in the field and I was just a first-year resident learning how to do colposcopy which is like looking at the vulva, vagina, and cervix through binoculars.

The thing is

when he stared inside that woman and I held her hand because I was just learning and when he said with the speculum inside the cold metal holding her open *well it looks like cervical cancer* my eyes met her wide open frightened eyes and I squeezed her hand and thought silently because I was only a small insignificant resident this is not how you tell a beautiful whole thinking feeling woman who is more than just her cervix that she has cancer this is not the right way to do that.

The thing is

when the faculty and residents and wives were at his house chatting and nibbling fancy cheese and fancy cakes and balancing little china plates and saucers without spilling and he snapped at his wife because she doesn't even know how to make a good cup of coffee and I saw the humiliation in her eyes but I was just a small insignificant resident so all I could do was share her humiliation in my heart and think this is not how you treat the woman (whether or not she makes a good cup of coffee you could make it yourself god damn it if you have so many opinions about fucking coffee) the woman who has stuck by your side and washed your underwear and made your bed and raised your children and put all those little delicacies in circles on that expensive china this is just not the right way to do that.

## Residency

*1975–1979*

*Beth Israel Hospital,*

*Boston, Massachusetts*

## In the beginning

when I got the letter
I made a very brash move.

called this prestigious
       exceptional
              researcher
                     creator of the (Manny) Friedman Labor
                       Curve.

told him
*Dr Friedman I was just accepted at Yale*
*if you don't take me at Harvard today*
*I'm going to THE COMPETITION.*

      (at Yale I would be the first woman resident
      in the history of the universe
      in obstetrics and gynecology
      the men all had crew cuts
      supported the Vietnam War
      and probably wouldn't like me one bit
      plus I would have to move to
      New Haven)

he took me.

now at Harvard I was one of four women
in the history of the universe
accepted at Beth Israel Hospital in obstetrics and gynecology
there were two ladies
two years ahead of me
two my year.

men who went into ob-gyn in those days
were often frustrated surgeons
couldn't get into surgical residencies
which really meant not the cream of the crop (if you get
      my drift)
surgery being one of the top crops.

plus there *were* benefits to the field.

the patients
        all women
                the nurses and staff
                    all women
                        the male doc was
                            king of his little female
                                fiefdom.

he ruled.

I worked with residents who were mostly smart
leaning towards arrogant
with varying doses of sexism
as well as kindness and generosity
mixed with outrageousness.

some doses were higher than others.

there was one guy
last name rhymed with *schlub*
(Yiddish for clumsy, stupid, unattractive, just saying)
known for doing a vaginal exam while eating a ham sandwich.

okay, I'm not sure it was ham.

but you get the idea.

then there was the day in labor and delivery
when (*schlub's*) scrubs had a hole in the crotch
he was not wearing underpants
so guess what fell out when he put his foot up on the bed
while examining the panting groaning woman between her
      contractions?

I know I should have said something
the nurses and I debated whether we were obligated
to inform him of his costume malfunction

(we were united in a sisterhood of struggle and subversion)

we decided
not
to.

that was spiteful.
but any thirty-three-year-old guy
who drives around in a pink Cadillac
teaches his little girl to bat her eye lashes and say
*My daddy fixes ginas*
deserves a bit of ridicule and hostility.

he left the program after one year.

some men perished on their own
went into radiology
were replaced with (hallelujah) women
maybe we were all a breath of fresh air.

they called us *Manny's Angels*.

our clinics were always filled with patients looking for
(young spunky) women doctors
mostly, our patients
loved us.

on the first day of residency
I was shown the Nurses Change Room
which was a narrow closet off the coffee room
in labor and delivery
piled with shoes
a tangle of hangers, clothes
the smell of sweaty feet, dried blood.

the Doctors Change Room was down the hall
clean
neat rows of lockers
a desk with a phone

a private bathroom connected to another room
with a bed and a desk.

not right.

I decided to change in the Doctors Change Room
which upset a number of older gentlemen
who did not expect to see a half-naked young woman
stuffing her foot into blue scrubs
as she hurried to get sign-off from the previous shift.

they got used to it.

I had less success convincing attendings
that it was not acceptable to call all their patients
*girls.*

obstetrical patients were sent to two floors
clinic patients on eight
private patients on seven
effectively segregating the floors.

obstetrical redlining.

no one seemed concerned.
it was
            how
                things
                    were
                        done
then.

I was trained by several decent caring docs
liberal-minded
supporters of the right to abortion
skilled surgeons
who took me on
like father/daughter
wanted me to succeed.

but still

it was a man's club.

## The outrage

a very jovial well-liked attending
on occasion came to the operating room
slightly drunk.

a popular doc
performing a vaginal hysterectomy
his beeper chirped
a patient was about to deliver upstairs
        (he should have asked someone to cover for him)
but he turned to me

        *Keep operating, I'll be back.*

dashed out of the room
returned twenty minutes later
scrubbed in
finished the case
the patient never knew.

one hyper-agitated attending
forehead beaded with sweat
wouldn't let me touch anything in the operating room
because the patient was a lawyer
he feared a malpractice suit
as he cut directly into her bladder.

oops.

another time he was in such a hurry
he couldn't wait for the scrub nurse
to get his gloves on
he did a dilatation & curettage grumbling
bare-handed.

an attending operating with me and
a chief resident on his
very difficult case
sat down on the floor
of the operating room and

cried when he couldn't
control the bleeding.

a doc refused to believe this wife-of-a-doctor patient
was in preterm labor
said it was kidney stones
forbade me to examine her
stayed in his office.

when she started feeling like pushing
I examined her and her cervix
was fully dilated.
he raced to the hospital
inserted forceps around the premie's delicate head
pulled.

the forceps
                came out
                without
                        the....................
                                        baby.

baby popped
into his hands
he cut the cord
held the tiny critter up for the mom to see
as it squirted out of his slippery palms
shot up over the mom's knee
she screamed

        *you dropped my baby!*

I leaped into the air
caught the kid
landed on my bottom
in a puddle of blood and amniotic fluid
screaming

        *I caught it I caught it.*

shit show took on a whole new meaning.

an oncology fellow and I
prepped and draped the patient

her legs supported by stirrups
took our positions
tucked against each thigh
the esteemed cancer specialist
strode in
dried his hands.

as he gowned and gloved he said

>     *We're gonna cut that pussy off.*

when I was a chief resident, an elderly very prominent doctor
was operating long past his expiration date
he was a kindly old-school gentleman who couldn't see
the sharp from the dull edge of the scalpel
made *his women* do an enema the night before their routine pap
    smears
took a woman to the OR for a pelvic mass that was her tipped back
    uterus
which was supposed to be there after all
once said to a frail 80-year-old lady lying in a bed
in front me of me and an eager medical student

>     *Spread your legs honey, I just want to take a cheap feel.*

DEEP BREATH ON THAT ONE.

I could feel the shame and vomit rising in my throat.

those were the days when the good old boys
all protected each other
played golf together
probably went to synagogue together
Beth Israel being for years the only hospital in Boston
where Jews could get admitting privileges.

I WAS NOT A GOOD OLD BOY.

I didn't play golf.

after four years, we three chief residents
(who were now all women)
marched into the department chief's office

stated quite clearly we would not scrub on cases with doctors
who were working past their expiration dates.

it was not our job to protect patients from
incompetence or
old age.

the elderly very prominent doctor reported me for *insolence.*

at his next case in the operating room
our department chief came down
took a brief look at the shenanigans and ended
the elderly doctor's illustrious
career
immediately.

the chief of the department revolutionized obstetrics
    used data rather than hearsay and habit to define the progress of
       labor
           forbade mid- and high-forceps deliveries because
              they could
                  cause neurological damage to babies
                     operated with a delicate grace in the
                        Germanic style in which he was
                           trained
                              could fix any broken body in
                                the operating room

terrorized the residents with his brilliance, sarcasm
and willingness to publicly humiliate

everyone.

## My most traumatic memory

the hysterectomy began uneventfully.
(despite my trepidation)

I was on the right, the department chief on the left
the errant uterus between us
the patient thankfully asleep.

residents peered over our shoulders
eager to see the great man in action
glad they were not me.

I was facing a clampless hysterectomy
a technique I had never done before
with the one doc in the world capable of performing the procedure
flawlessly.

thick tortuous blood vessels fed the uterus on each side.

I was doomed.

the chief elegantly threw in two silk stitches (in the old Germanic style)
        tied two secure knots around the vessel
                cut between them
                        handed me the suture.

I threw in two silk stitches
        tied two secure knots around the vessel
                cut between them
                        blood gushed into the pelvis.
                        the scrub nurse handed me a clamp
                                I grasped the vessel as the chief suctioned the
                                blood muttering under his breath.
                                the bleeding stopped
                                        I threw in another stitch or two or three
                                                handed the suture back to the nurse
who handed the chief a new suture.

we proceeded attacking each vessel in this manner
sweat seeping down my sides

a look of anger and disgust visible in the chief's black eyes
a thunder cloud gathering on the horizon.

L-I-G-H-T-N-I-N-G finally struck.

> *WHAT IS WRONG WITH YOU?*

> *ARE YOU MENTALLY RETARDED?*

tears collected at the edge of my eyelids
dribbled into my mask
slightly fogging my glasses

(fracturing my never-cry-in-the-OR rule)

*don't let him break me.*

I took the suture and started again.

valiantly.

another resident, my friend and buddy
chided the chief.

> *You know, yelling at her doesn't help. That's really not necessary.*

(she was older, used to work in the governor's office
'til a Kansas tornado sucked up her PhD thesis
and she decided to go to medical school
plus she was the mother of three young children
and could say things like that)

he looked up, laughed.

> *Just trying to light a little fire.*

or was he just
trying
to make
a real man
out of
me?

a woman<br>
surgeon<br>
healer

survivor
fighter
but not

a man.

# Triple F

*1976*

*Residency Clinic, Beth Israel Hospital*

*Boston, Massachusetts*

the chief resident nodded knowingly at the exam door
    *A Triple F.*

FAT, FERTILE, and FORTY.

a package of unappealing risks
unplanned pregnancies
chromosomally abnormal babies
diabetes
high blood pressure
uterine cancer
obesity.

all bundled up in one unattractive patient
a woman burdening us
with her care.

> I tasted the bile in my throat
> felt the clench of my jaw
> the anguish and rage in my heart
> crystalized.

on that day
I officially
unambivalently
became

a feminist.

## The There Down There

*1975 to 2013*

*Boston, Massachusetts*

over each exam table
a poster, a frog splayed across a branch
taped to the ceiling with the words:

> *All progress comes from taking*
> *uncomfortable positions.*

my most important gynecological instrument
after the potholders on the stirrups
the heating pad for the metal speculums
was the
mirror.

80-year-old grandmas
hoisted themselves up
on the hard exam table
peered over trifocals
as I adjusted the mirror, the light, the angle
looking
down there
for the very first time.

giggly teenagers
called it *My Pussy*
or *My Virginia*
as I named
each part of
the there
down there.

curious virgins
the traumatized
the eager
amazed
gay

straight
queer.

a plastic speculum
a mirror
a flashlight.

and it's all yours.

## Trauma Diminished

*1975 to 2013*

*Boston, Massachusetts*

caring for the abused, molested, injured, exploited
hurt, assaulted, touched
by fathers
brothers
uncles
family friends
partners
priests
doctors.

one woman disassociated during her pelvic exams
squeaking in a high-pitched child voice
reliving some earlier hell.

one woman shaking in tears
spoke of her father and brother
taking turns raping her when she was a child
with a pistol she always feared might
blow.

one queer woman had an appointment
with a homophobic doctor
who mercilessly shoved a cold speculum
into her soul
talked about how she just needed
some good sex to turn her around.

pelvic exam?

first

    talk in a chair with clothes on
        for as long as it takes.

then

    sit on the exam table with clothes on
        talk
            for as long as it takes.

then

    take clothes off

        if and when ready

           talk

                for as long as it takes while filling
                your lungs with long slow
                breaths and filling your body
                with relaxed open muscles
                sometimes counting
                backwards inhaling and
                exhaling every ten beats helps
                and sometimes a dab of local
                anesthetic helps too.

if and when you are ready and the speculum is warm and you can
    watch with a mirror
(if you want you can put the speculum in yourself or I will help you)

slowly

slowly

slowly.

together we say hello to your cervix, smiling back at you.

## Damages

*Boston area*

*1970s to 2000s*

we started couples therapy.
(it was a time of invention and self-awareness
avoiding the pitfalls of traditional marriage
pushing boundaries
exploring demons)

hoping we could improve and deepen
our relationship.

a gestalt therapist
soft bulky pillows
piled on the floor
spider plants hung
in macramé sacs
like sprays of tiny green fireworks
a color pallet of comfort and safety
promising insight.

the Very Radical Boyfriend wanted an open relationship
smashing exclusivity
challenging authority.

I was unsure
never craved the white dress
        diamond ring
                    daddy handing me over
                            to the next powerful man in my life.

but giving up monogamy?

we had our power issues
I was the pleaser
a good listener
he was more
the sensitive new age man
challenging sexism

the rules and greed of capitalist society
but still strong-willed
used to the white male son-of-a-doctor dominance
he had (uncomfortably) inherited.

I started individual therapy too
same shrink
mother issues
boundaries
power
depression
who am I?
>a girl with big ambitions
>big self-doubts.

one session, I fantasized my mother
was a huge boob shoved against my face
suffocating me.

the therapist grabbed one of those big pillows
pressed it over my face
until I couldn't breathe
panicked, it dawned on me that my quiet flail
muffled protests
were not working.

I had to fight
really fight
with fists
SCREAMING
SOBBING
ridding myself of
my suffocating mother
finding my strength
my loud
formidable
voice and
physical power.

that felt really good.

but the boundaries
in the individual sessions
began to blur.

some were clearly talk therapy
some drifted into hugging, soft warm lips
touching
touching.
(I only paid for the therapy ones)
it was complicated.

individual sessions continued
until I ended up in the therapist's
warm and welcoming bed.

seemed like a good idea
seemed like what I desperately wanted
seemed like the answer
to my lonely broken horny self.

but (of course) it wasn't.

for months afterwards
I searched for a female therapist
every *no, I'm sorry*
a personal rejection.

too few of them
too many of us.

years later
(after much more therapy)
I went to his apartment
to charge him with damages done.

his young daughter
waited to be picked up
by her now divorced mother.

when the front door shut
behind them
an uneasy silence settled
like the eerie stillness

before the roar of a tornado
touching down.

I exploded in rage
using my strong
formidable
(leaning towards fierce)
feminist
voice
hurling my pain
in his face.

emptied of grief, violation, confusion.

he said he was sorry
which was not enough.
(I still wondered, was it sort of my fault?)

even though I knew
a therapist must keep his hands to himself
NEVER take his pants off
with a patient
EVER.

after that
I tried to avoid
touchy kinds of shrinks
worked on undoing
the damage of that first encounter
amidst the crowded carousel
of family baggage.

one shrink
held me while I wept
which was confusing.

another
a friendly guy with comfy padded leather chairs
reminded me we were in med school
together
admitted he had a crush on me
grabbed my hand at the end of a session

after a deep relaxation exercise
working on my panic disorder

and KISSED my fingers.

I broke, fled
didn't get further than
sobbing in his waiting room
wounds still deep
hurling me backwards.

was it me?
was it something I said?
did I have some pathological seductive power
over therapists?

we talked
I yelled
he said he was sorry
which was still
not
enough.

decades later

I had a patient
who came for her pap smears
and a variety of sexual concerns.

she desperately wanted
to sleep with her analyst.
(women told me these kinds of things)

her mother had
she was their child.

trauma and confusion
passed in the DNA
from mother
to daughter
now stuck
bewildered
by unresolved yearning

and fucked up
boundary crossing
therapists.

I listened
understanding more
than she could possibly
imagine.

## The Bed Spread

*1975 to 1977*

*My bedroom*

*Allston, Massachusetts*

he took his stuff
half the down-payment on the house
most of my self-esteem.

I took to weeping
the nightly gouging out of my insides
anointing my private space
with doubting nothingness.

my        loveless      empty        life.

          (animate only in service
          only performing
          only living through the real      lives    of      others
          distracting me)

when my exhausted sorrows finally withered enough
that I could breathe without choking
I packed up the old platform bed
lugged the concrete blocks out
stacked them against the trash cans
tossed the damaged wounded mattress
          (stained with semen, menstrual blood, diaphragm cream,
                salty tears)
a graveyard of burdened detritus.

on impulse
bought myself a shiny expensive
art deco antique
brass bed.

took up crocheting
with long fat needles
thick ropy yarn
all oranges, browns, blacks

autumnal colors
readying like a bear
for the long lonely winter.

sitting cross legged
on that golden bed
nightly twisting and hooking each long row
a skinny belt emerged
a thick scarf
a clunky throw
a heavy bedspread gradually crawled
up from the shiny brass feet
toward my pillows
as I wove my emptiness
      back and forth
            back and forth
                  back and forth.

until I covered myself
shrouded in a cocoon
of grief and possibility.

# When Suicide Felt Like a Reasonable Choice

*1976 to 1979*

*Boston, Massachusetts*

we played too close to the edge
the Very Radical Boyfriend and me
until I couldn't do it
         anymore.

a moth singed by flames.

moving back to Boston
after my internship
to the old commune
I started residency that same week
the first day assigned to three months of night call
     six days a week
         fifteen hours a day.

that summer I staggered home in the mornings
the lawnmowers and screaming neighborhood kids
snatched away my desperate sleep
while he coasted
     tried to figure things out
         dabbled in relationships in New York
both of us pushing the boundaries of
monogamy and commitment.

the more desperate and needy I grew
         the more he wanted his freedom.

how many relationships survive medical school and internship
   anyway?

I threw him out of my life
in the office of a kindly therapist
who didn't know what to do with our explosive devices.

two moths singed by too many flames
hurting
     hungry

         angry
                 scared.

he said

    *what did I learn from you?*
    *I never want to be*
    *in an intimate*
    *monogamous relationship*
    *ever again.*
    *ever.*

was I that awful?
why didn't he just
slit my throat?

condemned.
unlovable.
unwanted.

by day, I was Wonder Woman
a smart, hardworking resident
at the hospital, 6 a.m.
brimming with smarts and competence.

getting home
in the evening
or the next morning
or often late the next afternoon
tired beyond tired
I found myself curled on the floor
between bed
and wall.

weeping.
    wishing self-harm.
        all used up.

I should have stayed at work.
quiet moments were playtime for demons.

alone with myself
I

was
nothing.

depleted.

I kept my desperation hidden
like an abscess brewing under my skin
threatening to kill me.

for years I survived
glued together
by an assortment of shrinks
who excavated my wounds
guided me out
of the shadowed gloom
        self-doubt
                self-hatred.

until
still a little crazy
but sturdy and
self-aware
I gathered my forces,
ready to take another chance
on

love.

# Jesus and the Wise Men

*1979*

*Beth Israel Hospital*

*Boston, Massachusetts*

Chantel had deep mahogany skin and wide black eyes
Chantel was twelve
Chantel was pregnant.

her grandmother with the large breasts
a wooden cross planted severely between them
was not pleased.

she prayed for salvation and guidance.

Chantel was twelve
when she saw Jesus and the Wise Men
in the parking lot overlooking
labor and delivery.

at her C-section
       severe toxemia
       small pelvis
       child-mother
she cried

       *I can't breathe!*

no one believed her
because she was often hallucinating.

when she stopped breathing
the anesthesiologist called it

       *A high spinal*

and promptly intubated her.

at her six week postpartum check
she asked for an IUD.

(she had her moments of sanity)

now she was an emancipated minor
because she had been
       foolish?
       irresponsible?
       victimized enough?
to get pregnant.
at twelve.

a very strange law.

when her grandmother with the heaving bosom
large dignified hat
Bible in her purse
found out

she threatened to kill me.

I told her

       *Your granddaughter wanted something.*
       *I could not refuse.*

# Meltdown

*March 1979*

*Antigua, Guatemala & Harrisburg, Pennsylvania*

fingers of scarlet molten rock
    zigged
        zagged
            down
the slopes of Volcán de Fuego.

a nightly eruption visible
from the high narrow window
in my bedroom
in my homestay
in Antigua, Guatemala.

Spanish emersion school.

otherwise known as
speak (medical) Spanish
or die
in five weeks.

it was a close call.

    *¿Como estas?*
    *¿Cuando fue tu última menstruación?*
    *¿Estás embarazada?*

my accent was decent.
grammar? *Muy embarazosa.*
the conjunctive?

impossible.

after school, I studied
memorized
struggled
bent over notes
sitting in my homestay
surrounded by an extended family

cooking pans of *pimentones rellenos*
for the local hotel.

renting out rooms
to students
who needed to practice
talking
with real people.

at night the ground shook
my bed
danced with the *temblores de tierra*
the earth gods teasing me.

do I hold on for the ride?
dive under the mattress?

evenings, I dragged
my heavy wooden dresser
against the door
a precaution after the *abuelo*
sat too close
on the couch in the living room
and put his hand on my inner thigh
while I was conjugating verbs.

a rapid nighttime escape would be difficult
under these circumstances.

in the morning
the whiff of eggs sizzling in hot oil
a lightning fast
cold-as-ice shower
fried *huevos* with fresh corn tortillas
sliced avocado melting on my tongue
Instant Nescafe with
sweet condensed milk.
(I guess they exported all their real coffee *al norte*)

   *¿Como estas?*
   *Muy bien gracias.*

my dedicated teachers
patient beyond reason.

> *yo voy*
> *ella va*
> *ellas van*
> *nosotras vamos.*

conversing with us
like giant toddlers.

> *¿Como estas?*
> *Estoy muy bien, gracias.*

one night
a *profesora* disappeared forever
they said it was
union organizing.

I worried.

what did they do to her?

I worried when I jogged
in the sunshine
brushing past bougainvillea
spilling like pastel
        pink
             purple
                  rainbows,
                      over high stucco walls.

past golden Spanish colonial churches
frilled like wedding cakes
cobbled streets
crayon box houses
      orange
           pink
                blue.

I worried
past the Mayan women in the market place
their woven
      fabrics

        bags
             skirts
                  hats
exploding with lush
    reds
        greens
            yellows.

a gringo in shorts
a tee shirt?

just asking for it.

I worried when I walked home
from the central park
stars glimmering
after savoring a *Gallo cerveza* rimmed with lime.
(careful never, never, ever to drink the water)

relishing crisp *pupusas* stuffed with chicken and pork
an evening at the movie theater
*Vasolino! (Grease!)* dubbed into Spanish
John Travolta strutting across the screen
his lips slightly out of sync
the electricity blinking on and off

like a weird dream sequence in s
             l
              u
               r
               r
              e
               d speech.

    *¿Te sientes mejor ahora?*

walking back to their homestays
girls were known to be
raped
alone
in the dark

on those charming
winding streets.

        ¡Horrible!

would I be next?

back home on the east coast
March 29 at 4:00 a.m.
near Harrisburg Pennsylvania
a cooling circuit malfunctioned
a release valve stuck
a cascade of mechanical failures
led to a partial m
                e
                 l
                   t
                    d
                      o
                        w
                          n of reactor number 2.

Three Mile Island Nuclear Generating Station
released a large poof
of radioactive contaminant
into the sky, earth, water.

the worst nuclear power plant accident
in US history.

I felt so relieved
to be
safe
in a tiny
Central American country
without
nuclear
reactors.

but still

I worried.

## Malpractice Suit: Expert Witness

*Late 1970s*

*Boston, Massachusetts*

the court chambers
smelled of old wood
and anxiety.

I stepped into the witness stand
the oak railing rubbed smooth
the judge draped in black robes
like a statue above me
the defense lawyer
pacing
readying for the kill.

I felt prepared
alert.

> the latest research on the Dalkon Shield
> the hot new IUD on the market
> with high rates of pelvic infection
> infected miscarriages
> infertility.

data marched back and forth
in my brain
like a flashing marquee.

the sad details of the patient's medical record
> haunted me.

breathe.

the prosecutor's advice

> answer only the question asked
> stick to the facts
> do not volunteer anything
> do not get flustered
>
> breathe.

I was in courtroom disguise
shielded by my dark blue suit
pearl earrings
hair tucked neatly
in a bun.

> I am an expert.
> I am credible.

> I believe injured patients
> deserve to have doctors
> who speak on their behalf
> in a court of law.

> (the prosecution had to settle on a resident like me)

> docs had a code of silence about testifying
> against each other.

*So . . . you were a baby*
*when the alleged incidents occurred?*

> No sir, I was an adult.

*An intern?*

> I was an intern.

*Not a real doctor.*

> I had my MD. I was a real doctor.

smirk
eye roll to the jury.

*You-were-a-baby.*

*You're being paid to say this. Right?*

I stared directly at him.
> As are you.

it went downhill from there.

I only remember
the waves of

        humiliation
             rage
                  fear
as I endured his legal strategy.

        belittle
        demean
        shame
        convince the jury
        ignorant little girl-doctor masquerading
        as expert witness
        what does she know?

we won the case.

years later, the doctor who lost
the malpractice suit
(that left his patient infertile)
tried to block my getting hired
at a practice in town.

I had violated the rules of the club
he remembered.

they hired me
anyway.

# Having it ALL

*1979 to 1988*

*Urban Woman and Child Health, Inc.*

*Jamaica Plain, Massachusetts*

an urban practice
located on the first floor
of an apartment building
for senior citizens.

a trolley rattled by
past a gas station, a funeral home
drug store, pizza parlor on the corner.

a non-profit with
a community board.

we were finally in control of our lives
(we thought)
in control of how we practiced medicine.

> no men at the hospital
> offered us jobs
> in their upscale practices
> women partners were not considered
> a selling point
> yet
> plus they thought
> we were too much trouble.

> maybe even a threat.

two women obstetricians
a pediatrician
midwives, nurse practitioners
a private office
three health centers
we tried to serve everyone.

and loved it.

> Insured, Medicaid, Medicare, self-pay
> sliding scale

no pay
barter.

health centers paid $24 per hour
Medicaid $4 a prenatal visit
private patients subsidized everybody.

we struggled to cover our costs
our own meager salaries.
two pediatricians joined us.
it was hard to hire
other obstetricians
the pay, too low
the call, too much
two health centers ultimately
went bankrupt
another big No Pay.

the waiting room quickly filled with
local Black and Hispanic families
white working-class folks
Cambridge feminists
from across the Charles River
suburban white ladies
looking for lady doctors
living in Wellesley and Newton
YUPPIES
(Young Urban Professionals
the vanguard of gentrification)
lesbians
folks with cerebral palsy
paraplegia
avoiding pregnancy
pregnant
menopausal
everything in between.

opening day
the toilet overflowed.

I scrubbed the floor myself.

one night when the electricity blinked
refrigerator failed,
the pediatrician raced over
to rescue our vaccines
from oblivion.
appointment times were generous
in the beginning
every woman was given
a copy of *Our Bodies Ourselves*
the Bible of the feminist movement.

we were committed to supporting
educating
healing in its broadest sense.

our cheerful, frenetic office
manager had
a psychotic break
her desk filled with unpaid bills
we discovered when our beepers
stopped working.

she never got through sending out
patients' bills either
free care from R to Z.
we were very popular
the only all-woman ob-gyn practice
in the Boston area.

working directly with pediatricians.

(we catch 'em
and toss 'em to you)

everyone brought their hopes
dreams
fantasies
demands.

one patient with a huge fibroid uterus
stared at me angrily
*How could you recommend a hysterectomy?*
*You're a feminist!*

            another did a double take
            when she walked into my office
            *You're not Black!*

we taught classes
offered backup for home births which were
shunned and belittled
by the mainstream establishment
spent long hours in the hospital
supporting women in labor.

thrilling, exhausting, sisterly work.
            not cost effective
            from a business point of view.
patients loved the midwives
            the hospital refused to give them
            privileges in labor and delivery
            until the month we closed
            eight years later.

            when the baby's head crowned
            one of us docs
            would rush in
            hang discretely behind the curtain
            while the midwife attended the
                delivery
            the doctor sent the bill
            signed the birth certificate.

we were mostly young women
professionals and staff
supportive of our own pregnancies
parenting
a three-month maternity leave.
(a very radical policy)

at meetings, someone was always
pumping
spraying warm milk
from overflowing, congested breasts.

over eight years
we had ten babies
that was just the docs
and the nurse practitioner.

        the hospital staff
        our former mentors and supposed
            friends
        refused to help with maternity
            coverage.

        not part of the old boys' network.

        I was told our patients were *too*
            *challenging*
        translation: poor, needy,
            outspoken, knowledgeable.

        ob-gyn malpractice
        skyrocketed to $85,000 per year
        per obstetrician
        that was the reduced rate
        for Harvard docs.

        we always said we would close
        when our malpractice was more than
        our salaries.

as usual
we had no role models
we defined our priorities
as doctors and working mothers
admitted our fears
self-doubts
supported each other
mourned together.

        our receptionist had a
        bouncing baby boy
        cherub cheeked
        thick, soft Afro
        died of SIDS

open casket at the funeral
a lacy white cradle
holding a silent, dead baby.
this was much harder than we had imagined.

I played
doctor, surgeon, psychiatrist
social worker
office manager
plumber
colleague
mother
wife.

on call mostly every other day
and night
our lives dictated by our
beepers.

my daughter used to yell
into her plastic red phone
*Just push it out!*
played meeting
with her stuffed animals.

when a mouse at school
had babies
my partner's son shouted
*Labor and delivery!*

we were controlled by
when women went into labor
ruptured their ectopic
        pregnancies
(Friday nights)
had their miscarriages
when my kids got ear infections
needed stitches
when the office flooded
or the abusive boyfriend
of a health assistant
arrived in a rage.

our work style made us unique, original
especially good for women
and families.
                but personally
                and financially unable to survive.

                the sobering reality was
what made our practice so successful
                ultimately led to its demise
                we were a small business after all
                with no business skills
                this was capitalism
                healthcare driven
                by profits
                payors driven by dollars
                not quality or creativity.

                every other night-call was tough
                especially when pregnant
                and vomiting
                (for nine months
                twice)
                or nursing a baby
                who refused to take a bottle.

                at night in labor and delivery
                or in between office sessions
                or surgical cases
                if I had a break
                I would rush home
                feed her
                rush back
                to work
                a whiff of breast milk and baby burp
                on my clothes.
I was having it all.

our patients gave us
a huge goodbye party
at Larz Anderson Park.

I still remember the photo
surrounded by piles of goofing, smiley kids.

our babies.

# Val

*December 11, 1980*

*Newton Centre, Massachusetts*

my ob-gyn partner and I
huddled together in the ethereal, stained-glass light
of Sacred Heart Church
cloaked in the smoky scent of
frankincense and myrrh.

mourners squeezed hands, hugged shoulders
witnesses to the unimaginable
weeping in the austere rows of dark pews
caught somewhere between thunder-struck
and disbelief.

Valentina Donahue
prodigal daughter of a proud ambitious Brooklyn nurse
wanted her child to become a cancer surgeon.

she did.

graduate of Barnard College and Harvard Medical School
Director of Gynecologic Oncology, Beth Israel Hospital
Gynecologic Oncologist at the Sidney Farber Cancer Institute
Assistant Professor, Harvard University
trained in pathology, surgery, ob-gyn
super-smart, talented, gorgeous, admired, loved
sometimes scatter-brained, but always focused
on the patient in front of her
the woman's well-being.

there were only two other women docs in our department
but Val was the one
we aspired to.

I wanted her surgical chops
her deep well of kindness
when faced with a frightened woman
staring at a cancer diagnosis

her ability to be brilliant, sexy
unintimidated by men.

one day she didn't show up
for a morning surgical case.

rumor spread like wildfire.

Nervous Breakdown.

eventually, they let her work during the day
return to some protected facility at night
we knew she was newly married
but understood little of her private life.

on December 7, her office nurse found her
a deadly assortment of empty pill bottles on her desk.

she was thirty-nine
seven years older than me
her fall into the abyss threatened
my steady march along the edge
now erratically cratered.

yawning, threatening, beckoning.

many of her patients came to my office
devastated, needy, afraid
looking for women doctors who would listen and care
we had been in practice for one year
each patient was accompanied by Vals' handwritten medical notes.

some women would start the visit with

> *You're not gonna commit suicide, are you?*

>> data: doctors commit suicide
>> more than the general population.

>> women doctors do it a whole lot more.

would I?

# Self Fiercely Mine

*1980s to 1990s*

*Boston, Massachusetts*

Suzanne escaped in her electric wheelchair
knees-fused-straight
twisted hand grasping the joy stick.

freedom chariot.

born with cerebral palsy
              locked in a closet as a child
                            sexually abused
                                          by her father.

Suzanne landed at the Center for Independent Living
churning with frustration
and dreams.

              an apartment
              her own space
              a life.

I cared for her at the office
the sweet powdery hospital soap
scent of her body
arms flailing
words like marbles
rolling across her tongue
translated her broken words
into will
              desire
                            demand.

her penetrating blue eyes
defiantly determined
to tell me how
to arrange her legs
manage her urinary catheter

honor her
self-care.

Self!

# Self!!

## Self!!!

her personal care attendant
got her pregnant.

twice.

was that love or abuse?

lifting her out of the chair
laying her in bed
        (was he tender?)
spreading her legs
doing it.

I did both her C-sections
lifting the infants
out of her uterus
into a strange uncertain future.

       (she couldn't push a baby out
       could she hold one?)

she felt happy.
she made a healthy family.
she was a mother.
she loved her children.

Fiercely!

# Fiercely!

## Fiercely!

I would see her downtown,
scooting along the sidewalk
a kid on each outstretched leg
dusky blond hair flying in the wind
wide smile

a staccato wave
that look of vulnerability and defiance.

*Don't underestimate me.*

Mine!

Mine!

Mine!

# Oral Boards

*1981*

*A fancy hotel*

*Chicago, Illinois*

fortified with coffee and Imodium
my deranged gut
seething with anxiety
I wait in a sea of anxious men
in a much-too-small room
for my name to be called.

dark suits everywhere.

I obsessed over the critical female question
what to wear?

demure but intelligent
not too threatening
white blouse with a curved collar
lady-like thin red scarf
grey wool jacket
blue skirt
legs shaved
pumps
small stud earrings
a dab of lipstick
loopy curls tucked in a bun.

a cross between librarian and missionary.

we each are led
down corridors
(like rats in a maze)
to our own test sites.

an ordinary hotel room
where I face a microscope
a pile of pathology slides.

*Name The Organ And The Disease Process.*
*This Section Will End In 60 Minutes.*

I stare at the inviting double bed
the small square radio.

force myself to focus focus focus.

an hour later
a famous professor clicks open the door
he brings a slide projector
with medical histories
electronic fetal monitor tracings
X-rays, clinical dilemmas.

he can ask me anything.

I want to ask him:
do you remember that I was the first woman
accepted to your residency program
in the history of the universe
and *I* turned *you* down?

focus focus focus.

an hour later
two rotund, congenial, southern gentlemen
review my case list
every surgery I have done for the past year
(I am a surgeon after all)
my successes and complications.

they can ask me anything.

they do.

do you plan to marry?
do you plan to have children?
will you be able to practice medicine?

DING-DING-DING.

brain racing
I could sue the pants off of you
which would not be pretty.

I smile demurely
formulate my strategy
like a general
in the throes of battle.

oh no, I nod sweetly
I plan to devote my life to medicine
I am a nun in the service
of the goddess of the uterus.

I document everything.

months later when I am officially
accepted as a Fellow in the
American College of Obstetrics and Gynecology
I lodge my complaint.

the official Letter of Apology comes quickly.

they know I could sue the pants off
all of them.

# Modern Love

*June 3, 1982*

*Cambridge, Massachusetts*

we eloped at 11:00 a.m.
in the dark chambers
of the Justice of the Peace

> no god
> no obey.

toasted with champagne
on the sloping lawn of Cambridge City Hall.

> THE FOLLOWING ANNOUNCEMENT
> DID NOT APPEAR IN THE BOSTON GLOBE

> *The bride wore a cotton blue kimono shirt*
> *Black velvet pants*
> *A bouquet of roses and irises.*
> *The groom wore a vaguely Mexican shirt*
> *Embroidered with red and yellow flowers.*
> *The bride's parents*
> *Were really pissed*
> *They were not invited.*
> *The groom's parents*
> *Were just happy.*

I didn't want to be
given away
father-to-husband
human trafficking.
I
belonged
to
my
self.

I didn't want a silky white dress
like a pure virginal offering
to a man I would honor and obey.

I didn't want
an argument with my mother
about rabbis, prayers, rituals, floral arrangements.

that morning I jogged three miles
to Memorial Hall
and back
washed my hair
blew it dry into a sweep of
lion's mane.

ready.

I was bursting with desire for
an equal partner in life
fellow deep-sea diver
adventurer
co-conspirator.

didn't really need
a marriage license
(or a driver's license
hunting license
how-to-live-my-life license)
to define my commitment
and love.

he did
(for the children yet to be born)
so we did.

three-day honeymoon.

our green van shaving-creamed
JUST MARRIED!
cars honked all the way to
Cape Cod sand dunes.
            in the rain
                    smoked weed
                            savored lobster
                                    inhaled the perfume of roses
                                            laughed at the sky.

a month later
we moved into the old commune house
second floor apartment.

August pregnant!
first time we set our minds and bodies
to THAT.
          so surprised
                    so so happy
                              so so so lucky.

we were sprinting
everything about
to
unfold.

wet wings of a butterfly
stretching out of the cocoon
          drying in the sun
                    readying to take
                              flight.

# Downs Baby

*June 1983*

*Beth Israel Hospital*

she draped her leg
over my swollen belly
(the only way I could get
close enough to deliver her baby—
I was due any minute)
her husband stood on the other side
holding her as she pushed.

she had a dream pregnancy
amazing labor
I felt excited
almost envious.

after the head emerged
I wrapped her hands around the baby's shoulders
together we lifted the boy onto her belly.

mother and father curled around their child
weeping with relief and joy.

I looked
knew at once
broad forehead
almond shaped eyes
flattened bridge of the nose.

the nurse knew too.

Downs Syndrome—Trisomy 21—intellectually disabled.
(this was before
routine prenatal screening
blood tests
ultrasounds)

I called in the pediatrician
a wise gentle soul.

he explained that the baby
was beautiful
had well-formed arms
chunky little legs
ten toes
ten fingers
a perfectly formed belly
a strong heart beat
a very kissable baby.

the parents glowed and cooed.

and probably
Downs Syndrome.

silence.

the father recoiled
shocked
never touched his baby again.

the mother wrapped herself around her infant
and cried.

the next morning
I waddled into their room
the mother-in-law
lunged at me screaming

*How could you let this happen?*
*I could kill you!*

her son had to restrain her.

they decided to put the baby up for adoption
(there are families that adopt Downs babies)
the husband told his wife she had to choose.

they left together
empty-handed.

two weeks later
I was wheeled into
my postpartum room.

I could hear my roommate
through the blue checkered curtains
a big adoring loud working class Italian family
smells of garlic and tomato sauce
blue balloons bouncing off the ceiling
a baby boy.

broad forehead
almond shaped eyes
flattened bridge of the nose.

they could only see
what was beautiful.

now it was my turn
to weep.

# My Turn

*June 29 to July 1, 1983*

*Boston, Massachusetts*

forty hours of labor started at midnight and went on forever and
a year which is a
very
        long
             time.

the first twenty-four, I sat in a wooden rocking chair, breathing
easy, soaked in the old tub with lions feet, walked and walked
until I knew every dust ball in the house, stayed hydrated,
hydrated, and more hydrated, hungered for scrambled eggs, (some
bizarre metaphor for pregnancy?) freaked out the electrician who
kept saying, *shouldn't we call your husband?*

I knew this was only the beginning.

(I was an obstetrician after all)

        baby, baby, baby, stirring in my belly doesn't want to
            leave
        I want to wrap myself around you
        on the *outside*
        get it?

after the morphine sleep which didn't quite work, (I was high *and*
my uterus contracted), the nurses called the sweet supportive but
really quite anxious husband back from his warm bed at home in
the middle of the second night and we started the breathing,
back-rubbing, walking, rocking all over again.

that afternoon, hot shower thank you thank you.

        baby, baby, baby stirring in my belly doesn't want to
            leave
        what is your problem?
        I've got roomy Russian peasant hips my mother always
            said
        were good for *something.*

Pitocin drip to make my loopy contractions more *effective* (which is a euphemism for extremely painful, especially the part about back labor which feels like the baby's head is an enormous jagged rock splitting me in half, chainsaw comes to mind)

> baby, baby, baby stirring in my belly doesn't want to leave
> why the hell are you doing this to me?
> have you no mercy?

finally finally ready to push

and push

and push

and push

eyes swollen, blood-shot, hair dripping wet, weary
hospital johnnie soaked in sweat and primal determination.

three-and-a-half long excruciating hours later
the little demon finally emerged face looking up (it's called the posterior position which is a form of cruelty for the laboring soon-to-be-now-wishing-she-was-kind-of-dead-cause-it-hurt-so-much mother).

baby was a little stunned, needed to be suctioned, a whiff of oxygen to pink up, a head so squashed I could see the deep impression of my pubic bone across her thankfully soft cone- shaped skull.

why was she so big inside and so little out here?

I was (deliriously) stunned too, (no amount of delivering other people's babies prepared me for *this*), glad the ordeal was over over over, no rush of maternal love, desire to hold the much wanted child just wanted to sleep.

she latched on with such ferocity my nipple split the first time and the life force let down in my body, I held her tenderly wondering who this strange apparition was, still filled with anger and resentment.

that night, floating in a daze, confused about why the bed was so high, the toilet so low, my body so swollen and sluggish, wanting to feel something other than bewilderment

I cradled this perfect squirming girl, staring back at me, slightly cross-eyed.

those determined jaws already demanding more more more
a flood of sudden tears, a bolt of lightning
we both had survived
we were fiercely connected
colostrum flowed.

she didn't do this *to* me.
she did it *with* me.

passionate unbounded love flooded the room like a tsunami over my sore spent body and wrapped this girl securely in my aching newborn-mother grip.

forever.

# Parenting

*1983 onward*

*Boston, Massachusetts*

our first child
gave birth to her parents
slowly
but firmly.

she slept next to (or in) our bed
nursed
on demand
(for much of the day and night)
napped when she was tired
demanded company
entertainment
bouncing
singing
goofy frog faces
when she was not.

she was in our arms
tucked into various front and back pouches
papoose-like
the rest of the time.

> *They say your heartbeat*
> *the smell of your body*
> *are soothing to the infant*
> *warm memories of the womb.*

as soon as she could
she fed herself
streaked her hair with avocado
tossed spoons of yoghurt over her shoulder, *all done!*
fell asleep in her ravioli and tomato sauce.

> *So she needs a bath*
> *that's what water's for.*

when she piled her stuffed animals in a corner
climbed out of her crib
bounced off the change table
fell on her head
twice
we put a mattress on the floor
called it a bed.

(it was safer that way)

we honored every injury.

> *Don't say it doesn't hurt that much*
> *when it does.*
> *It's her body.*

gaggled over every accomplishment.

> *Wow. Finger painting.*
> *Kind of Picasso meets Jack Pollack*
> *don't you think?*

she picked out her clothes
perfecting the eclectic
glam hobo princess bag lady look.

> *Hey, if it's not a public health hazard*
> *what does it matter?*
> *She's dressed. It's a skill.*

our house gradually transformed
into a giant play space
kiddy library
game center
with gates at the stairs to limit head trauma
a huge mirror in the hall
for preening, dancing, making faces
the tall box from the new refrigerator turned hiding place, pirate
    ship
wedged next to the dining room table.

*I'm counting to three*
was about as harsh as it got.

we listened
we bargained
we tried to respect the world
as she saw it.

(within our human limits)

when number two was about to arrive
we read (all the right) books about
loving your sister
hating your sister
helping your sister

JEALOUSY
           FRUSTRATION
                      ADORATION
                                 COMPETITION

the new baby gave her books
soft green cotton pants
a matching shirt with flowers across the top.

the big girl
leaped into her big sister clothes
sat in a roomy hospital chair, holding the newborn
hugged her tight tight tight.

despite my weary
up-all-night labor
I beamed.

           *Such a mature child*
                      *so well prepared for a sibling*
                                 *so loving.*

she looked up and said
"Is she dead yet?"

           *Better to say those things than act on them, right?*
           *So in touch with her feelings.*

imagine her surprise when she found out
I had forgotten to tell her
when I came home with that baby

and we all snuggled in as a new family
I was planning to stay home for a while.

with NUMBER TWO.

number one was going back to preschool.

she was not pleased.

they say it feels like an old lover
   being told
      when a sweet young thing comes along.

    *Oh don't worry. What's the fuss?*
    *I have enough love for both of you!*

just look at it from
her point of view.

doesn't seem fair, does it?

## Something to Prove

*1980s onward*

*Brookline, Massachusetts*

there was a magnet
on our fridge
a couple dancing
all debonair
and swirly skirt.

the caption read
Ginger Rogers
did everything
Fred Astaire
did
only backwards
in heels.

finishing the morning office in time
to pump milk from my bursting breasts
before electric pumps were easily available.
(pumping usually during staff meetings)

coaxing reluctant kids
into their clothes
out the door
without a meltdown.
(morning being a minefield
of reluctance and urgency)

rushing to daycare
at the end of the day.
(clutching unfinished charts
phone messages
pages of lab results
needing to get done
now)

managing an office
patients with pre-eclampsia in need of emergency admissions

older menopausal ladies with hot flashes driving them to despair
girls with ruptured ovarian cysts, ectopic pregnancies
urgent urinary tract infections
weary exhausted moms with postpartum depression
my anxiety in the operating room
post-call exhaustion

> the whispers in the back of my brain
>> women can't do this
>> women are too emotional
>> women aren't strong enough
>> women aren't smart enough

> always worrying
>> am I good enough
>> am I staying up-to-date
>> have I forgotten anything
>> anybody
>> anywhere
>> am I too distracted
>> will the kids be okay
>> does my husband even remember me?

you know what they say about working mothers.

the men all seemed to have wives
or secretaries
to take care of these things.

me?
I was just
dancing in those
heels.

backwards.

## Making it UP

*1983 to forever*

*Boston & Brookline, Massachusetts*

we set out to create something new
no role models
no parents we unambivalently admired
no raise our kids like *that.*

equal:
>parents
>cooks
>trash collectors
>nose wipers

though sometimes we specialized.

I
>supervised pediatric appointments
>immunization schedules
>squirted bright pink amoxicillin
>into reluctant mouths treating
>endless ear infections.

he
>cooked the majority of dinners
>(I was on-call or late coming home from the office)
>if I was home we always ate together
>as a family.

I
>negotiated with a chef
>who came once a month
>cooked up a pile of freezable meals
>all divided and labeled
>ready for reheating
>to lessen the load on Chinese takeout.

he
>took care of the house
>renovations

       leaky plumbing
       wood-burning stove
       lawn mowing.
I

       took care of the health and
       emotional well-being
       of the children
       who confided at night
       paged me by day
       with their distress, hurts
       fears, traumas.

through five pregnancies
three miscarriages
two children

he held my hand
humored my cravings
nested
as I threw up for nine long months
twice
puking in the morning, afternoon, evening
       between patients
             in the car rushing to the hospital
                at 4:00 a.m.
until the day I went into labor.

drove me to the hospital for the D&Cs
held me in my grief.

first time, I labored for 40 plus hours
in a blur of back pain,
endless, thunderous pushing
exhilarating, humbling, death-defying
childbirth.

the second
*only* eighteen hours
twenty minutes of pushing
still a lot.

he was there.

I nursed my sweet babies
(could have called them Jaws
for their passion and toothless grips)

but after the basic biology

we just loved those girls
  diapering
    feeding
      dressing
        reading
          tickling
            playing in the park
              kissing booboos
                rushing to the ER for stitches
                  frosting elaborate birthday cakes.

loved them inside
and out
loved them
some more.

I made more money (doctor)
his work was more flexible (woodworker)
I never worked fulltime
translation:
part-time: 50 to 60 hours per week

when you count
        office
           surgery
             charting
               on call
                 consults
                   conferences
                     lab follow-up
                       staff meetings.

we developed a complex spider web
of responsibilities and work schedules
taped a giant calendar on the fridge
      pick up

    drop off
    gymnastics
    more as they got older (piano, trumpet, dance, karate,
        basketball . . .)

taught our childcare provider
living in the downstairs apartment
how to drive
bought her a car
ever grateful for her steady love and commitment
to our family
always worried that someone would forget a kid somewhere.

    never did.

I knew
he would always pick up the pieces.

every now and then
we snuck off.

    booked a night in a downtown hotel
    a grownup dinner
    drank a glass or two of fine wine
    finished conversations (without interruption)
    saw a play (without Big Bird)
    reveled in a night
    (uninterrupted by little feet)
    shared kisses over eggs benedict
    delivered to our room.

by mid-afternoon
we were eager
to
go
home.

snuggle back in
with
the
kids.

we just
adored
those loving
            crazy
                    challenging
                            gorgeous
girls.

# Dr. Alice Rothchild's Subversive Rules for Pelvic Engagement

*1980s*

*Beth Israel Hospital*

*Boston, Massachusetts*

they came from all over the country
newbies and oldies
clinicians-in-between
wanting to update
their knowledge
at a Continuing Medical Education course
at Harvard University.

the latest on yeast infections
ovarian cysts
UTIs
ectopic pregnancies.

most importantly
to master

      The Dreaded Pelvic Exam.

the annual course was billed as
Gynecology for the Non-gynecologist
I was a clinical instructor
talking clusters of (sometimes) anxious clinicians
through the fundamentals
of the exam
and my idea of basic, respectful, human etiquette.

Dr. A's rules:
1. Meet the woman sitting up, human to human
2. Introduce yourself
3. Establish eye contact, warm but not friendly in a creepy way
4. Shake her hand
5. Do not tower over her, asserting your power, position in life, maleness

6.   Explain every move, as in
7.   *Please put your feet in these stirrups*
8.   *Scootch down* (I know I said scooch, is there a better word?)
9.   *Let your knees flop apart*
10.  *Now I'm going to touch your knee* (do not touch the vulva first, think about it)
11.  *Now you will feel my finger pressing on your vaginal opening*
12.  *Relax the muscle where you feel the pressure*
13.  Warm the speculum!!!
14.  *Now you will feel the speculum entering your vagina*
15.  Do NOT eat a ham sandwich, etc.
16.  And in real life: *Do you want to watch with a mirror? See your cervix?*

the best part of this exercise:
the "pelvic models" were educated young women
who worked in local women's clinics
were motivated to teach clinicians
how to do this in a sensitive thoughtful fashion.

so . . . as the hesitant/anxious/rough/confused
went through the rules of Dr. R.
they received instantaneous feedback.

> *Too hard, go slower.*
> *That's fine.*
> *Okay, you're touching my cervix.*
> *Did you feel that? That was my ovary.*
> *It popped between your fingers.*

> this deliberate reversal of power
> felt like reparations
> justice for all the sexist, insensitive,
> disgusting behavior
>
> women have endured.

# Circumcision

*1985*

*Newborn Nursery, Beth Israel Hospital*

*Boston, Massachusetts*

the only surgery I ever did
on the male species was
circumcision.

snipping the foreskins off
tiny penises
of vulnerable newborns.

an odd custom if you stop to think about it.

Jews evoked ancient ritual
Abraham clomping along on his donkey
chatting with God
who promised Abe's 99-year-old wife
Sarah
a son
a menopausal miracle.

Isaac.

Abraham, Isaac, and Ishmael
the son of Abraham's mistress,
(he was clearly a frisky *nonagenarian*)
were all circumcised.

a covenant with God.

genital marking
an ancient cultural ritual
celebrating who's in
(and who's out of)
the tribe.

Muslims agreed.

most Christians thought it was cleaner
less infections
less risk of HIV
less penile cancer.

but mostly
daddies wanted their sons
to look like them.

atheists and agnostics were ambivalent
as was I.

babies hated it.

one couple wanted to watch
and I, respecting the parents' wishes
agreed.

my first sense of trouble
was the look on the nurse's face
but I was cocky
sure-footed.
why not?

as I bound the baby's
arms and legs
with Velcro bands
spread eagled in a
plastic restraint
grabbed the foreskin
with a clamp
lifting it off the penis
the father hovered over his son
radiating anxiety.

as the baby wriggled and shrieked
I could feel the father's breath
he gasped and moved closer.

the nurse asked him to stand against the wall.

my hands started to shake
sweat trickled down my back
my heart thudded.

the nurse made the parents leave the room.

what was I thinking?

a woman cutting off a little boy's penis
even just a tiny bit.

Daddy watching.

I could hear Freud
laughing in his grave.

## Heart Sounds

*1980s*

*Urban Woman and Child Health, Inc.*

*Jamaica Plain, Boston*

a stethoscope laced my neck
black tubing gracing my collar
the bell warmed in my palm
pressed against soft downy skin.

heart sounds
valves closing with a turbulent
underwater plop
lub-dub lub-dub
sealing atria from ventricles
ventricles from aorta and pulmonary artery
the jangle of living.

breath sounds
the in- and ex-hale
air swooshing
deep into the nooks and crannies
of bronchi and alveoli
a tiny river of wind
gusting oxygen into the blood.

stethoscope
the symbol of my trade
my competence.

over time
I noticed the sounds
growing
fainter
and

f
 a
  i
   n
    t
     e
      r.

I feared deafness
or some as yet undisclosed brain disorder.

one morning
my stethoscope yielded
nothing.

I turned to my patient
to apologize for my failure
my incompetence
(my impending dread disease)
fearful I was not good enough
losing my touch
if not my mind.

she laughed.

     *Doc, there's a big hole*
     *in that rubber stethoscope tubing thingy.*

I stared
closely.

the vibrations had escaped
    bounced all over the exam table
       spilled onto my sensible shoes
          danced down the hall
             rushed into the wintry street.

when will I learn to trust
my own heart sounds?

# Noses

*1980s*

*Boston, Massachusetts*

my dermatologist shared an office
at the Faulkner Hospital
with a plastic surgeon
a doctor of nose jobs
rhinoplasty.

I was there for skin
itchy eczema on my fingers
strange freckles between my toes
plus she pierced ears
and our children took swimming lessons together
at the Y.

I had sort-of-come-to-terms with my
Jewish, too-big-for-comfort
curved the wrong way
nose
actually the least of my problems
when it came to the standards of
American womanly beauty
in the twentieth century.

photos? I instinctively
faced the intrusive camera lens
minimized the record of my flaws
gut sucked in
shoulders back
chin up
no profiles for me.

a shiny brochure sparkled on the desk
aglow with faces and perfection
ratios of forehead to chin
eyes to mouth
pages of ideal noses, perfect proportions, suitable sizes

notably narrow, with a slight upturn leaning towards perky
some with a touch of ancient Greek god.

(*rhino* meaning nose
*plasty* meaning shaping
in Greek)

this rhino doc
had no room for me
a real fixer upper
in his waiting room
no room either
for noses from South Africa, Cambodia, Mexico, Poland, Tahiti
lovely varieties of protuberant, flatter, wider, longer
he was all Anglo-Saxon
a white man's vision
of (female) attractiveness
available for a pricey fee.
(I bet he did chins and cheekbones too)

I sat there squirming
my hand casually placed
over my face
my fingers screaming with itchy bits
as shame washed over me.

suddenly
       humiliation
            morphed
                into
                    anger.

but then
I smiled
relieved that Rhino Man
       was never gonna put his
          wrong nose
              on my
                 right face.

## Falling Out

*late 1980s*

*Urban Woman and Child Health, Inc.*

*Jamaica Plain, Massachusetts*

a hunched up
owl of a woman
frizzy grey crown
lizard skin
years of too much sun
in El Salvador
the fields of California
back bent at harvest time
lifting sacs weighted with tomatoes.
(or whatever food we took for granted)

her daughter translated
actually, did most of the talking.

> *Woman troubles.*

I caught bits of the Spanish.

> *Mami, mami*
> *Dolor*
> *Presión*
> *Flujo vaginal.*

she confessed
(embarrassed)
something was falling out
*down there*
ten babies
had left their mark.

> *Is it cancer doctora?*

she had no language
for that hidden damaged female place
fearful

legs spread in stirrups
her face shrouded in her hands
moaning *Dios mío*
as her daughter patted her shoulder.

when had she last seen
a doctor?
nurse practitioner?
midwife?
had health insurance?
any preventive care at all?

diagnosis:
Total Prolapse
    cervix
    uterus
    bladder
    rectum.

her vagina twisted inside out
like a turned around sock
toe to heel
hanging between her thighs
her sad bleeding cervix
half way to her knees.

this trouble had not happened overnight.

how many years
had she suffered
    pain
      pressure
        bleeding
          discharge crusted in her underwear
            impossible struggles peeing and pooping
as she sweated in those fields feeding us?

another woman oppressed by
    shame
      ignorance
        fear
          a system rigged against her.

it didn't have to be this way.

I knew how to fix her body
but the system?

years of radical surgery
political vision and determination
for that.

# biggering and **BIGGERING**

*1988 to 2013*

*Boston, Massachusetts*

we always said
(joking)
we would close our intimate feminist Urban Women and Child
    Health
when our malpractice costs
were greater than
our salaries.

that took nine years.

by then we were
*desirable*
established women docs, midwives, nurse practitioners
with a busy ob-gyn practice
the world had evolved
in our favor.

we were wooed
Harvard Community Health Plan won the courtship
and our business.

HCHP, a large HMO
health insurance and health care
rolled into one
many kinds of salaried providers
under one roof
offices all over the city
forward-thinking
easy for patients.

riding the storms of the marketplace
HCHP mutated
into a sprawling group practice
gobbled up by other corporate entities
the big cats biggering and biggering.

I figured they knew how
to run offices
(that's what they did)
but I agonized
not delivering my own patients
the anonymity of a sizable medical practice
so many partners, so many styles.

twenty-four hour on-call only once a week
catching babies
treating women with ectopic pregnancies, preterm labor
all manner of troubles
sounded like a relief
but in that 24 hours I might deliver
eight squirming babies into this world
spend three days blurry-eyed
in recovery
as I powered through offices and surgeries and preschool pickup
never quite in the right time zone.

it turns out most of my partners
were hard-working women and a few men
the practice had solid values
a commitment to keep us educated.
(which it did)
growing professionally.
(which I did)

it turns out management was terrible
at running offices.
(much of that fell to us in the trenches)

it turns out that coming of age
when the behemoth electronic medical record
was being developed, tested, rolled out, reprogrammed, tested again
on our weary minds and bodies
was a near-death experience.

I spent more time typing and looking for
        billing codes
        diagnostic codes

drop downs
negotiating an exploding in-box
than working in the operating room.

(I went to medical school so I wouldn't have to type
be some man's secretary.)

I WAS SO VERY WRONG ON THAT ONE.

it turns out that practicing humane, thoughtful medicine
while the bean counters were counting
productivity the north star
insurance companies had a choke hold
drug companies spent more on advertising than research and
    development
budgets had to be met or else
was a deeply frustrating and enraging experience
that had little to do with health.

(how can I maintain eye contact with the patient while typing notes
    on a computer that is behind my back or do I save all those
    handwritten notes and enter them in the evening after my kids
    have had their baths and bedtime stories and the kitchen is
    cleaned?
plus I have to check all my new labs and review the charts for
    tomorrow and it's midnight and I'm cross-eyed with exhaustion
how do I do that?)

my partners and I hunkered down
our offices like little villages
a quirky family with drama, misunderstandings, joy,
    accomplishments
the hospital another intense community of friends and foe.

we did our best to maintain
the principles of our original practice
adjust to the business of medicine
shoulder leadership roles
take care of the women
who came to see us
despite everything.

humbling and sustaining work.

as we negotiated a healthcare system
with its own distinctly
American
corporate
profit-making
disorders.

# Nightmare

*late 1980s to early 1990s*

*Boston, Massachusetts*

> obstetrics is like cocaine
> the highs are very high
> addictive almost
> the lows are
> end-of-the-world
> awful.

we were expecting a bad baby which is to say a baby in distress gasping for breath heartbeat slow muscles limp—the heart tracing abnormal at admission to labor and delivery but all the fetal scalp sampling within normal range which is to say that likely something terrible had happened in the uterus (constriction of the umbilical cord? placental abnormality? heart problem? something else?) after the normal testing three days ago and the onset of labor this morning.

every time I considered doing a C-section the high risk ob docs said no it wouldn't improve outcome so the soon-to-be mother and father labored on knowing we were worried but not knowing how worried.

as the head crowned the assembly of sick-baby specialists hovered over the infant warmer arranging tubes for intubation oxygen drugs as my heart exploded and with a deep dread I urged the soon-to-be mother to push-push-push.

deadly silence as the baby emerged, awash in green meconium— baby poop mixed in amniotic fluid not always a bad sign but in this case thick mec and very bad—mom and dad craned their necks from the delivery bed eyes anxious over the cluster of doctors around the baby warmer like a swarm of industrious bees and no cry no cry just suctioning, the rustle of plastic, the nurse whispering come on baby come on baby.

intubated and already tied to heart and oxygen monitoring IV dripping—baby was whisked to the neonatal intensive care unit which was very high level but not high enough and then in an incubator and ambulance to Children's Hospital where the baby tried to die over and over kept alive on a heart-lung machine and the best of modern medicine.

I knew the heartbroken parents she was a social worker he was an early childhood interventionist I was their obstetrician and we agonized over the chart and fetal monitoring tracings and testing and the baby's stormy hospital course and we held each other in our grief and the shock of the unexpected catastrophe arriving like a thief snatching the end of a joyous pregnancy.

weeks and weeks later when the baby was ready for discharge the daddy said to me—

*I understood her lungs were damaged, but I didn't know it was her brain too.*

the parents chose to take the 24-hour-care-every-minute-of-every -day baby with minimal brain function home to love her and feed her and suction and monitor and worry worry cry—the marriage strained the father fell apart and we talked on the phone and held each other in our sorrow.

months later the parents transferred their beloved limp minimally responsive baby to a chronic disease hospital for children where she contracted chicken pox and died and we held each other again.

the mother returned to me for her second pregnancy which was complicated by a large ovarian cyst, a dermoid, which had to be removed at the end of the first three months of pregnancy since rupture could cause a miscarriage or premature labor so she came to the hospital—the scene of the deepest sorrow in her life—and realized the place was haunted and she could not stand to be there.

she told me regretfully she was transferring care to another doctor and another hospital and I understood completely.

I learned that when she was in labor again filled with more than the usual anxiety and dread there were some blips in the fetal monitor tracing nothing worrisome but the dad could not tolerate his fear and the docs did an emergency C-section for paternal distress and the baby was born healthy.

a couple of years later just before the end of the statute of limitations for legal action—I was served with a malpractice suit accusing me of gross negligence, malpractice, and other devastating heart-crushing charges.

> obstetrics is like cocaine
> the highs are very high
> addictive almost
> but the lows are
> end-of-the-world
> awful.

my insurance company chose to settle.

## Miscarriage

*Fall 1991*

*Boston, Massachusetts*

I was forty-three
long past hope.

for eleven weeks
I held on to that baby
held on
held on
held on
wrapped my strong
mother arms
my sturdy welcoming uterus
holding my baby
holding
holding
holding on
even as it died
inside me.

for eleven weeks
squinting into grainy ultrasounds.

the tiny sac
growing
growing
growing
too slowly
flickering heart beat
slipping away
slowly
slowly
slowly
last chance
chance
chances

slipping away
slowly.

after the D&C
sucked the last possibility of life
out of me
I awoke in the recovery room
woolly brained.

Anita Hill
was testifying on the
TV above my bed
something about
something about
something about
pubic hair on a coke bottle?
Clarence Thomas?
Supreme Court?
her earnest black face
the wall of old white men
doubting her
doubting
doubting.

I knew
deep in my grieving soul
justice looked
as broken as
I felt.

# First Panic Attack

*Fall 1991*

*Boston, Massachusetts*

still bleeding and silently bearing my losses
cocooned in my bed
dreaming
my beeper buzzed
      rattled
                wake-up-wake-up-WAKE-UP
startled, confused
I bolted into reality
the alarm clock glowering
three a.m.

groggy call
labor and delivery
secretary's urgent voice

      *Dr. Rothchild, a patient just arrived in active labor.*

*On my way.*
brain laser-focused.

I grabbed my underwear, slipped on a bra
threw a dress over everything
moments later my orange VW Rabbit
cruised along Storrow Drive
beside the languid darkness of the Charles River
a shimmering moon tossed in the hollows
of the water.

from the deepest recesses of my bereavement
my pulse bolted upward
heart banging against my chest
overwhelming doom crowded
into my consciousness
a struggle to inhale
a sense of impending death.

I slowed my car to a crawl
cranked the window open
the night breeze slapping my face.

doctor brain announced to cowering brain
*ALERT. Panic Attack.*
*Get Yourself Together.*

I pulled into a turnout
concentrated on
breathing
the urgency of the moment screaming
GO.

I started slowly
my foot leaded in quicksand
unclear if I could drive
under the nearby bridge
a sudden fear of tunnels and
hard-to-get-out-of tight dark places.

I turned onto a residential street
inched to the hospital
counting forwards and backwards
the radio loud
focused on inhalation/exhalation/foot-to-gas softly
talking to myself as if from
an extra-corporeal body.

as soon as I crept into the hospital parking lot
the fright subsided
by the tenth floor
I metamorphosed into myself
like superwoman in a phone booth
transformed
a well-trained doctor
(soldier, dancing circus bear)
warm, competent, in control.

the birth was lovely.

no one knew.

another patient arrived, baby distressed
I called a stat C-section without hesitation
minutes later I delivered the baby
tight umbilical cord
squeezed around his neck

no problem.

no one knew.

as the sun ascended
and the adrenalin rush drifted south
only then did I hear
the voice whispering like an unwelcome ghost.

*I cannot get home I cannot get home I cannot get home.*

my car and the task of driving now the embodiment
of all my anxieties
the trauma of delivering other people's babies
when I had lost my own
the focus of all my fear, grief
neatly compartmentalized
into a place and a task.

it only got worse
before
it got
almost
better.

# The Pap Smear

*1993*

*Harvard Community Health Plan*

*Boston, Massachusetts*

he came to the office
for his pap smear.

short sturdy build
baby boy mustache
            feathering his upper lip
alto voice trending towards
baritone.

transitioning.

I had never before asked a man
*when was your last menstrual period?*

the hormones made them
            go away
unplumped his breasts
lowered his voice
but he still had a uterus
and a pesky cervix that needed

a pap smear.

how did he feel
sitting in my waiting room
wedged between pregnant bellies
thirty-somethings needing
their birth control pills
scanning *People Magazine.*

women whose genders
matched up
with the sexual organs
they were born with.

how did he feel
filling out the medical forms
laden with binary language
assumptions
about who he was

or wasn't?

how did he feel
when they called his name
    and elderly ladies frowned
        teenagers looked up
           stared
                stared
                    stared.

I wanted him to feel safe
welcome.

he was my first patient
    to take testosterone
      to have surgery
        top and/or bottom
        or not
           to refuse
             to be

categorized.

I could have done better.

# Victoria

*Early 1990s*

*Boston, Massachusetts*

the first time she got pregnant
sweet lady from Haiti
with the charming husband
her uterus distorted by massive fibroids
she lost the baby at four months.

when the bleeding and grief
faded
to the place where she could breathe
without weeping
I took her to the operating room
opened her belly
cut out the offending muscle tumors
patched her uterus together.

try again.

the second time she got pregnant
sweet lady from Haiti
embraced by the consoling husband
she presented with severe high blood pressure
I scrambled to tame the monster
she lost the baby at five months.

try try again.

the third time she got pregnant
sweet lady from Haiti
held together by the resilient husband
her blood pressure carefully controlled
she developed severe pre-eclampsia
forcing me to deliver a premature girl
who chose
to live.

the fourth time she got pregnant
sweet lady from Haiti
adored by the happy husband
her blood pressure carefully controlled
I delivered a full-term, healthy girl.

they named her Victoria.

a week later
the husband found his wife unconscious
the baby suckling at her breast.

Massive Stroke.

had she forgotten her medications?
tired? depressed?
was this a rare postpartum eclamptic seizure?

the neurosurgeons charged aggressively to battle
cracked her skull
tubes out of every orifice
the click-click of a thousand ICU alarms.

they didn't explain much.

I took to visiting the sweet unconscious lady from Haiti
the distraught husband in the ICU
every day
holding him in his despair
translating her ominous surgical course
demanding clarifications from the busy neurosurgeons.

who didn't explain much.

when brain death settled in
the ventilator heaving and snorting each breath
fending off the inevitable
the blindsided husband arranged for her mother
a tiny wrinkled village woman living in Haiti
unused to airplanes
shocked by the icy cold of Boston winter
to arrive coatless in sandals
bewildered, wrapped in a scarf of anguish.

the priest was called
the family prayed and wailed
I shared their heartache
held hands, hugged shoulders
the ICU doc shut off the ventilator
her heart slowed to eerie silence.

many in the Roxbury Haitian community
attended her funeral
which was filled with loud singing
the flailing of grief laden bodies
beseeching and praying to Jesus.

I sat in the back
feeling very white
and very sad.

the US government declined to give the grandmother
papers to allow her stay in the states
help raise the children
so the bereft husband could continue to
drive his cab
buy groceries
pay the rent.

she returned to Haiti with those two babies
leaving him childless again.

years later
I spotted him in a market
with those two little girls
a new wife
a new life.

try again.

## The Right to Choose
### (version published *Writers Resist* 2021)

*December 30, 1994*

*Brookline, Massachusetts*

on December 29
twenty-two-year-old John Salvi
thick black hair
a wisp of a mustache
eyebrows knitted together
over the bridge of his nose
drove to a hunting range
to practice his aim.

the following day
less than two miles
from my home
on a crisp, subzero morning
forty pregnant girls and women
partners, friends, mothers
anxious, sad, frightened, resolved
waited in a Planned Parenthood Clinic
for their turn.

Salvi strode into the clinic
carrying a black duffle bag
if anyone had been watching
they would have heard the quiet buzz
as he opened the zipper
removed a modified .22 caliber
Ruger 10/22 semi-automatic rifle.

he hit the medical assistant, Arjana Agrawal
in the abdomen
killed the receptionist, Shannon Lowney
with a shot to her neck.

screaming, blood splattered everywhere
a scramble for safety

a hail of bullets
five wounded.

he took his gun
sprinted to his Audi
drove west on Beacon Street
two miles
Preterm Health Services.

Salvi strode into the clinic
asked the receptionist, Lee Ann Nichols
*Is this Preterm?*
shot her point blank with a hunting rifle
a security guard, Richard Seron
returned fire.

Salvi dropped the duffle
containing receipts from a gun dealer
in Hampton, New Hampshire
plus seven hundred rounds of ammunition and a gun
fled south to Norfolk, Virginia
captured after firing over a dozen bullets
into the Hillcrest Clinic.

police arrived at Preterm
five minutes too late.

I trained before abortion was legal
cared for women
traumatized, mangled, infected
by back-alley procedures.

I was an abortion provider
at the Women's Community Health Center
and Beth Israel Hospital
ten minutes from Planned Parenthood.

the next morning
my eleven-year-old daughter
asked me, as I left for work

*Mommy, are you going to die today?*

## Family Therapy

*1990s*

*Brookline, Massachusetts*

hoping to untie some twisted knots
in the gnarly roots
of our miscommunications and distrust
give grievances sunlight
just feel better.

my brother and I
started family therapy
with our mother.

intentions were good
plus I had some things
I really needed to say.
(in the presence of
a mediator
witness
interpreter)

at one point
the well-meaning woman
suggested we invite Dad.

(why was he missing
in the first place?)

he came
uneasy.

after the let's-get-comfortable chitchat
therapist lady turned toward him
respectfully.

> *Mr. Rothchild, this is a safe place*
> *let's stop and think*
> *what would you like*
> *to say to your daughter, Alice?*
> *this is your opportunity.*

I listened
expectantly
with the slightest twitch
of hopefulness and
curiosity.

he smiled blandly
a handsome smart
used-to-being-in-charge
supports-his-family-generously
pillar-of-the-community
weeps-when-he-listens-to-Mahler
kind of guy.

shook his head.

> *Alice is always so busy*
> *I really don't have anything to say*
> *to her.*

I glared at the therapist.

why is it always my fault?

sadly
she was not skilled or adept enough
to negotiate the tricky pathology
lurking in my family.

\*\*\*

what I should have said
would have said
could have said.

(had I not learned to be silent
like him
had I ever perfected the art
of fighting back)

> *Dad*
> (looking straight into his eyes, unblinking)
> *I will not take responsibility*
> *for your emotional absence.*

*own it.*

*say something*
*say anything*
*for Christ's sake.*

*if your mind draws a blank*
*(is that really what goes on in there?)*
*how about*

*I don't know you*
*I don't understand you*
*I don't approve of you.*

*but I will always love you.*

*try that one Dad*
*just try it.*

I didn't
of course
he didn't
either.

# Just Another Doctor's Office

*1990s to 2001*

*Boston & Brookline, Massachusetts*

when my office renovation was completed
freshly painted in soothing colors
tenth floor, Copley Square
the building reflected
in the adjacent Hancock towers.

I could gaze out my window
see my tiny twin face
trapped in a 62 story skyscraper
a multifaceted mirror of office windows
floating in blue sky
like a scene from a
Charlie Chaplin movie
about capitalism and
cogs in some massive money-making industry.

I invited my father
to come see the place
(feeling proud and excited)
lunch at some upscale restaurant
tex mex? seafood? nouvelle cuisine?
you pick
connect over medicine or work or
something
anything.

his off-the-cuff reply.
(thought
less)

> *Why would I do that?*
> *It's just another doctor's office.*

stunned silence.

words trapped
howling inside me.

an internal tornado.

> *fuck no, Dad*
> *it's not any old office*
> *it's mine*
> *mine*
> *your*
> *daughter's.*

> *I'm inviting you*
> *to a show and tell and*
> *chat*
> *remember chatting?*
> *we sit and talk and eat*
> *you know*
> *it's called having a relationship.*

we never met for lunch.

a decade later
stalked by death
befuddled by alzheimers
dad lay skeletal
in a rented hospital bed
wheeled into my old bedroom
gaunt, disappearing
his toes curling up like bird claws
my mother spooning chicken soup
into his dry mouth
he grasped my hand
as my brother and I rubbed
morphine on his gums
his voice raspy and desperate.

> *Alice, why can't you fix it*
> *Alice, why?*
> *fix it, Alice, fix it.*
> *why can't you fix it?*

my mother
(deranged by grief)
lit into her three children
after she heard
us chuckle.
(a morbid, tension-release
could-this-get-any-worse
kind of eruption)

she accused us
of laughing at him.
(which we were not)

turned her fury on me.
(see deranged by grief
but still speaking inner truth)

accused me of terrible misdeeds
cruelty
never giving him
a chance
destroying our relationship
a disgrace
a failure
a monster of a daughter.

damned.

my brother and sister stared open-mouthed.

steeled with quiet fury
(slightly deranged by my own grief
no more chances
this is all we got)
I told my mother

(emboldened by years of therapy)

> *Dad was*
> *emotionally absent*
> *drifting into actively disapproving.*

*now he is dying*
*I am doing my best.*

*if this is not good enough*
*for you*
*I will pack my stuff*
*walk out the door*

*and you will never ever see me*
*or your grandchildren again.*

*I refuse to be blamed*
*for everything that went*
*wrong.*

she stomped out of the room.

reappeared later
shaken
scared
angry.

*you can stay.*

# PART FIVE: THE GRAND FINALE . . . SO FAR

In which I reach some level of uppity clarity and some level of outrage and despair.

# Worth Fighting For

*1960s to now*

*United States*

## Imagine

IMAGINE: you are fourteen, raped by your uncle, pregnant.

in 1971, to obtain an abortion in Massachusetts
you had to prove the pregnancy was
a threat to your life and mental health
convince your gynecologist
> two psychiatrists
>> the chief of the gyn department
>>> or a hospital abortion committee.

some insurers only paid for an abortion if the woman was married.
you're fourteen, your parents don't know
how're you gonna pay?

a total of six states and Washington DC permitted legal abortions
*in some circumstances.*
> over one million *illegal* abortions were performed
> *every* year in the US.

IMAGINE: you are twenty, in college, condom broke.

pregnant women
traveled to New York (if you had the cash)
where abortion was legalized in 1970.

> there was a plane
> for women in Detroit
> who needed abortions
> flew direct to Buffalo
> doctors bundled the costs-
> the flight was included in
> the price of the procedure.

by 1971, there were almost as many abortions
as babies born
in New York City.

that same year, President Nixon announced
his opposition to abortion
at any time during pregnancy
based on his own *personal and religious beliefs.*

IMAGINE: you have five kids, no money, period is late.

without the availability of legal abortions, frantic pregnant women
    tried
        herbs
            malaria drugs (quinine, chloroquine)
                poisons and dangerous liquids (turpentine, bleach
                    detergents)
                beatings
                    throwing themselves off stairs or roofs
                        poking coat hangers, knitting needles
                        bicycle spokes up their vaginas
                        into their uteruses
                          back-alley butchers.

city hospitals had *septic abortion wards* filled with severely ill women
thousands died of hemorrhage and infection
the death rate for non-white women was twelve times higher than
    whites.

women of means found sympathetic docs or traveled to countries
like Sweden.

in the 1950s, New York City, abortion ratios divided by class and race.

safety could always be bought.

in the '60s, small groups of women, (civil rights activists, feminists)
organized to provide
trustworthy, reliable abortions.

in Chicago, the Jane Collective provided 11,000
safe, illegal abortions

before they were accused
of multiple
felonies.

# THE LAW

(according to mostly white men who have never been pregnant
but want to sleep with their women on demand
and may or may not be willing to use
a condom
or take responsibility for the behavior
of their sperm)

(why is Lady Justice always blindfolded???)

1965: Griswold v. Connecticut, Supreme Court overturned a
Connecticut law that made it a crime for a woman to use birth
control devices or to ask a doctor to prescribe them.

1971: United States v. Vuitch, Supreme Court rejected the claim
that the District of Columbia law permitting abortion only to
preserve a woman's life or health was unconstitutionally
vague deciding that "health" included psychological
and physical well-being.

1972: Eisenstadt v. Baird, Supreme Court ruled that married and
single women had a right to buy contraceptives and the law
could not be used to limit distribution based on marital status.

1973: Roe v. Wade, Supreme Court ruled that the US
Constitution protected a woman's right to privacy—and her
right to choose abortion before the pregnancy was viable.
but . . .
the abortion right was not absolute.
it must be balanced against the government's interests
to protect women's health and prenatal life.
in the second trimester
the state could regulate abortion.

1973: Doe v. Bolton, Supreme Court ruled that the right to
privacy included marriage, pregnancy, contraception, family
relationships, child rearing, and education
broad enough to include a decision to carry or terminate
a pregnancy.

1992: Planned Parenthood v. Casey, Supreme Court affirmed
the right to abortion
before viability, stated abortion restrictions unconstitutional
if enacted
for the purpose of creating obstacles to abortion.

2021: Whole Woman's Health v. Jackson, Supreme Court
rejected a request to block enforcement of Senate Bill 8,
a Texas law
which prohibited most abortions after six weeks of pregnancy
with no exceptions for rape or incest.
enforcement delegated to private citizens who in effect become
bounty hunters encouraged to sue anyone involved in an
abortion
for $10,000.
2022: final appeal shut down.

2022: Copycat bills to the Texas Senate Bill 8 and worse appeared
in
Idaho
Ohio
Florida
Missouri
Tennessee
and more.

2022: Dobbs v. Jackson Women's Health, Supreme Court ruled
that the constitution
does not guarantee a right to abortion.

June 24, 2022
folks took to the streets
marching, chanting, weeping
in outrage and disbelief
as the "pro-life" movement
rejoiced.

by 2024: Twenty-one states banned abortion
or restricted the procedure earlier in pregnancy
than Roe v. Wade
twenty-seven states upheld the right to abortion until viability.

current estimates: half of US women
(and queer non-gender conforming people with uteruses)
will lose access to
abortion services
that's 33 million living breathing thinking fucking
reproductive age humans.

anti-abortion arguments are often based on a rigid reading
of the US Constitution
which was (after all) written by
cis gendered heterosexual white landowning male slave holders
(who really understood women).

you could say
in 2022
people opposed to reproductive rights
seized control of the uteruses of people who have them.

you could say
an embryo has more rights than a grown person
that privacy and physical autonomy
is no longer a woman's right
that women
and queer people with uteruses
will bear the consequences of
contraceptive failure, rape, incest
unconsented sex
per usual
that a gun owner has
more rights than
a woman.

you could say
that women and queer people of color
who have the least access to health care
contraception, a living wage
now
will have even less.

you could say
that women and queer folk

will suffer and die because
docs are afraid to
terminate miscarriages
end nonviable pregnancies
remove ectopic pregnancies
while there is still a

heartbeat.

(in the fetus)

New consent form for abortion procedure:

Abortion is a very safe procedure. The risks include infection, bleeding, perforation of the uterus, incomplete removal of tissue, however your greatest risk is. . . . Prosecution.

# Let's Be Logical

how about a vasectomy for every man
who creates an unplanned, not-ready-for-this
didn't-really-mean-it
kind of pregnancy?

worried about his future unborn, preborn
not yet fertilized progeny?
no problem.

we'll just round up all the culprits
have a big jerk off party at the Supreme Court
save their precious tadpoles in a million tiny glass vials
plopping them is some mega freezer
then defrost the sleepy wigglers when each man is
mature enough
committed enough
ready enough
has signed enough forms
to assume the full responsibilities of
fatherhood.

I mean, he was really asking for it
did you see how tight his jeans were?
Christ, you could almost see his manhood
the way he strutted his pelvis on that dance floor
did you notice how much he drank?
utterly irresponsible.
got what he deserved
what a tease.

that'll teach 'em a lesson.

2022: Supreme Court Justice Clarence Thomas
wrote that gay rights
gay marriage
contraception
are next
on the Conservative let's-destroy-America

throw-women-(and LGBTQI folk)-
back-to-the-early-1800s
dystopian chopping block.

when I had my *pregnancy scare* in 1969
my crazy boyfriend sold his motorcycle.
(as I agonized over my looming catastrophe)

just in case we needed the money
to . . .
you know.

# Things I Have Learned About Blackness

*1619 to now*

*Everywhere*

my Black psychotherapist with the fabulous fro
kind, empathic eyes
lanky, graceful body
always wore a running suit
while jogging
to reduce the chances of being stopped by
the (mostly Irish) Boston police.

that was a clue.

running while Black could be dangerous
even with a PhD.

many medical students and docs
(falsely) believed
Black people don't feel pain like whites.
*(thicker skin, fewer nerve endings)*

docs tended to
listen more closely to white people
took their pain more seriously
did cardiac workups quicker
recognized their faces more easily.

that's even documented
in the medical literature.

I rarely heard anyone explain
that neighborhoods where Black people
have been allowed to live
are often close to
              polluting industries
                          toxic waste facilities
                                      chemical plants
far from fresh food markets
              green parks

drowning in liquor stores
and a thousand daily micro-aggressions.

that world produces a body on alert
stress hormones on the ready
fight or flight
wrestling for a little bit of turf
a little bit of *mine.*

always on the lookout for
*the man.*

the legacy of slave women
forced to nurse their owners' children
while their own went hungry
that hurts too.

could make a healthy person sick
and it does.

Blacks are poorer
have more asthma, high blood pressure
kidney disease, obesity
more pregnancy-related complications and death
breastfeed less.

not a defect in the gene pool.

*race* (a social construct)
is not a risk factor.

people are sickened by
redlining
school to prison pipelines
environmental inequities
police brutality
chronic stress
*racism.*

no easy prescription for that.

# Things I Have Learned About Women

*always*

*Everywhere*

The word *hysteria*
derived from the Greek
*hystera* or *womb*
denotes a wandering of the womb
a longing for children.

Hippocrates
Greek physician
460 to 370 BC
the *Father of Medicine*
recommended marriage
as the best remedy
for female insanity.

so this kind of shit
goes way back.

when a woman is strong
smart
ambitious
aggressive
she's a bitch.

a man?
successful.

if you think
we've come a long way baby
just look at what they're selling us
impossibly thin models
with perfect airbrushed faces
peddle stuff to fix
our imperfections
disgusting smells, oily skin
unruly hair, hips, breasts.

there is nothing about a woman
that cannot be improved by a product
or a surgeon's knife.

we are defined by our inadequacies
marketed and focus-grouped to death.

an early ad for Premarin
an estrogen replacement medication
for menopausal women
featured a handsome, older woman
grey-haired
high cheek-boned
holding a dead rose
with the inscription:

*For the symptoms that bother him most.*

back in the bad old days
my airline stewardess patients
starved themselves before
each regular weigh-in
authorities checking to be sure they were
thin
and
attractive
enough

*to keep their jobs.*

there is no such thing as a *routine pelvic exam*
when 25% of women have experienced
sexual assault.

tee shirt: The Patriarchy is Not Going to Smash Itself.

what can I say?

AGITATE!

# Woman

*always*

*Everywhere*

There is no simple way to name a
person-who-may-or-may-not-have-ovaries-whose-gender-
is—female.
A person who-may-or-may-not-have-lived-as-female-since-birth-
but-knows-who-they-are now
and/or doesn't-identify-as-particularly-binary in a world that
categorizes everyone in boxes male/female.
There is no simple way.

a dash of introspection
about the word
WOMAN
(aka lady, girlfriend, wife, mother, goddess, temptress, mistress,
    whore, bitch, cunt)

female icon ♀

goddess of love, beauty, desire, sex, fertility
Rome—Venus
Greece—Aphrodite.

noun—woman

from the Old English *wīfman*
*wīf*: woman or wife
*man*: human being or man.
[woman not quite human unless with man]

a word loaded with submission
        social place
                expectation
                        peril
in a male society.

a term long tied to gender assigned at birth.

feminists in the 20th century (me)
tended to be inspired by
white heterosexual womyn

wrestling for equality
emancipation from the male gaze and male supremacy
embracing our gay sisters
but often blind to the lives of

transgender
queer
nonbinary
questioning folks

and womxn of color.

decades later
my sisters, brothers, and everyone in between
dynamited open my shuttered brain.

let some nonbinary
cross-border startling sunshine

sparkle in.

# Obstetrical Musings

*Just after Eve and forever more*

*Everywhere*

a pregnant person is crammed
with underappreciated
organs.

the placenta with its thick, ropy blood vessels
glistening in the dark
rooted to the walls of the womb
like a great, life-giving beech tree.

the cervix, a tight-fisted neck
molded to the southern end of the uterus
a pink mouth with many faces
tight, puckering, pouting, laughing out loud
holding the baby in
then magically
(with the help of prostaglandin and a whole lot of effort)
letting her out.

the vagina, a narrow tunnel
with such versatility
squeaking in tampons
warm and moist for penises
and other pleasures
stretching like a giant balloon
around the baby's bowling ball head.

secreted hidden splendors
shrouded in obscurity.

PENIS ENVY?

forget it.

# PART SIX: UNADULTERATED, UNAPOLOGETIC HERSTORY

In which the origins of outrage are revealed.

# The Not So Benign History of Head-Shrinkers and Black People

*1700s–2000s*

*United States*

you will find
the history of racism is central
to the history of psychiatry.

in my youth
I nearly became a shrink.

years later, I'm still doing
all kinds of psycho
analysis.

poking around the conscious and unconsciousness
of the child—named psychiatry
living and growing up
in the messy intolerant
cultural/political brew
that is US history.

try sympathetic head nods
the occasional *uh huh, I hear you.*
sit back in our comfy leather chair.

WARNING

crazy lies in the convictions of the beholder.

## Session one

*shall we start at the beginning?*
*people have been anxious*
*depressed, delusional*
*forever.*

*hidden away*
*restrained*
*tortured*
*accused of being possessed*
*shamed for moral and spiritual failings.*

we were secreted
in family homes, madhouses
prisons, asylums, hospitals.

*what have we here?*
*a lithograph from colonial times*
*half-dressed men and women*
*hallucinating, writhing in anguish*
*on a dirty stone floor*
*shackled to the walls.*

doc, there were other treatments
dunking in ice baths
mummifying patients in wet cloths
spraying naked crazies with water
submerging them for days
purges
bloodletting.

*intimidating the insane into*
*cooperative behavior?*

exactly.

1773—first patients admitted to
the Public Hospital for Persons
of Insane and Disordered Minds
Williamsburg, Virginia
the earliest US public institution
exclusively for care of the mentally ill.

*the patients?*

white patients got first dibs
free and enslaved Blacks next
slave owners paid for the care of their chattel
slaves could also be accepted as payment
for care and treatment
enslaved patients were hired out
to work in private homes.

*treatments?*

the troublesome ones got
padded cells, solitary confinement
food passed though iron grills
filthy beds of straw.

*Black people?*

1792
"negritude"
a condition described
by Dr. Benjamin Rush
father of American psychiatry
claimed the color of Black people's skin
was a mild form of leprosy
claimed he turned a Black man white
by vigorously scrubbing his skin.

*really?*

Rush believed
mental illness was caused by
blood vessel irritation
best treated with bleeding, purging
hot and cold baths, mercury
and his favorite
the tranquilizer chair
ankles, wrists, body, head
locked into place.

"It binds and confines
every part of the body.
by keeping the trunk erect
it lessens the impulse
of blood toward the brain."

*which relieves blood vessel irritation?*

right.
also the gyrator
a spinning contraption
that disoriented and
nauseated patients.

*ahhh.*

## Session two

*good to see you again*
*tell me about insanity.*

John M. Galt one of the founders of
the Association of Medical Superintendents
of American Institutions for the Insane
(precursor to the American Psychiatric Association)

one of the heads of the
Williamsburg Virginia asylum

didn't expect Black psych admissions
thought insanity was a disease of the "civilized."

Africans and their descendants were
too primitive to be crazy
white people suffered from
the mental excitement of
daily decisions and responsibilities.

Blacks were "immune to insanity
because they are removed from much
of the mental excitement
to which the free population
is necessarily exposed
in the daily routine of life."

*(so who's crazy now?)*

*I mean, what kind of stress*
*could possibly come from*
*being bought and sold*
*having your children ripped away from you*
*being raped and beaten with impunity*
*living under the total control*
*of your master?*

agitated patients were treated
in cage-like "crib beds"
six feet long
eighteen inches high

three feet wide
slatted coffins.

or tightly swaddled in
full body canvas coats
strait jackets
often tied to chairs.

*so these are hospitals and asylums?*

overcrowded, understaffed
the results of the 1840 US census
had a new category "insane and idiotic."

it was interpreted to reveal
higher rates of insanity among
northern Blacks than southern slaves
used as a defense for slavery.

"It is a mercy to him to give this guardianship
and protection from mental death."

*I can hear the pain*
*in your voice.*

John McCune Smith, the first Black person
licensed to practice medicine in the US
and Edward Jarvis, a physician
father of American biostatistics
disagreed with this analysis
publicly and vehemently for decades.

*BIG HEAD NOD FOR THAT.*

## Session three

*can we look again*
*at the question of*
*race?*

prominent psychiatrists
were ardent segregationists
believed insanity was caused by
worry and anxiety.

*therapy?*

Moral Treatment
books, fresh air, healthy food
strolls in lovely gardens.

keeping the upper classes
away from the stress of
associating with lower classes.
(read Black people)

*so what happened to Black people?*

Blacks were diagnosed with "drapetomania"
"a disease causing Negroes to run away"
1851 Samuel Cartwright thought slaves
who exhibited an obstinate desire to be free
suffered from this peculiar form of
mental illness.

*uh huh.*

he also diagnosed
"dysaesthesia aethiopica"
a troublesome physical/mental ailment
described as a poor work ethic
skin insensitivity and
dulling of mental faculties
prevalent in freed slaves

but also seen as "rascality"
in those still in bondage.

best treated by washing, oiling
whipping the skin
and "some white person
to direct and to take care of them."

*deep sigh.*

for decades prominent psychiatrists
pathologized, demonized Black people
called them "primitive, savage
unfit for life as an independent citizen."

asylums became violent overcrowded
prison-like institutions
long rows of locked rooms.

a hand reaching through
the small square window.

a patient lying half-naked
chained to his bed.

outbursts led to days
naked in a dungeon.

*(I am weeping silently.)*

uniformly segregated
by color and class
men from women
screamers from silent sufferers
violent from curable.

the colored institutions were
poorly funded, congested
Black patients forced
to work in the fields.

they were some of America's
first officially
segregated
institutions.

*we have to stop.*

*that's all for today.*

## Session four

*then what happened?*

>1895 Black doctors established
>the National Medical Association.
>(the American Medical Association
>was segregated.)

>Howard University, Meharry Medical College
>other black hospitals, medical schools
>provided education and training
>Black docs, nurses, and students
>began the long effort
>to desegregate medical institutions.

*that sounds like*
*a whole lot of shame to deal with*
*a whole lot of challenging assumptions.*

*demanding action.*

*a whole pile of truth telling.*

*what happened when drugs*
*and surgery were invented?*

>at the end of the 19th century
>drugs and surgery
>began to replace
>physical restraints.

>insulin shock
>electroconvulsive therapy (ECT)
>became popular.

>followed by prefrontal lobectomy
>brain surgery that
>cut the connections between
>the thalamus (emotion)
>and the frontal cortex (thinking).

>leaving an emotionally flat dulled
>easily controllable
>(damaged) person.

*that was considered a success?*

yup.

by the 1950s
control and possibly treatment
were achieved through the use of
psychotropic drugs.

*got it.*

*lest you think racism is long ago and far away*
*the present is haunted by the past.*

by the 1970s
the diagnosis of psychosis
and schizophrenia
was given to Black men so often
as to be a description of
aggression and agitation.

distress was conflated with anger
depression underdiagnosed
antipsychotic drugs overused.

Black communities were described as
"seething cauldrons of psychopathology"
behavioral symptoms included rioting
participating in civil rights protests
being very very angry.

then crack cocaine hit.

*highly addictive free-based cocaine?*
*aka crack?*
*aka rock?*

entire Black communities were
criminalized.

*the treatment for addiction?*

incarceration.

1974, ad in the "Archives of General Psychiatry"
a Black man raises his fist
defiantly
"Assaultive and belligerent?

Cooperation often begins with Haldol."
[a powerful antipsychotic]

by the 1980s with the closing of asylums
and the rise in prison population
jails became . . .

*holding pens for the mentally ill?*

that's right doc.

*I think our 50 minutes are up.*

but wait
I'm not done.

man, this isn't over
Black people in mental health crises
restrained
medicated
tasered
shot
at higher rates than whites.

I'm not done!

*I understand.*
*we will talk about this next week*
*and the week after*
*and the week after*
*and the week after . . .*

## Session five

back in 1903, W. E. B. Du Bois wrote
in *"The Souls of Black Folk"*
"How does it feel to be
a problem?"

> *no wonder*
> *people of color*
> *do not trust*
> *head-shrinkers.*

> *like I said*

> *crazy lies in the convictions of the beholder.*

# An unauthorized, outraged feminist history of childbirth and doctoring in America (totally biased because I think women in general are smart, strong and by the way have been having babies since just after Adam and Eve bit the apple and Mr. Snake wriggled out of the Garden)

*Always*

*Everywhere*

## Doctor Knows Best!

let's be real
midwifery
prostitution
the two oldest
professions for women.

women have always been healers for whatever ails
from the spirit to the womb
from lust to labor
the herbalists, abortionists, counselors
primordial scientists dispensing advice, folk medicine
empirically through trial and error
mother-to-daughter, neighbor-to-neighbor
wise women to some
witches, shamans, and charlatans to others.

it has always been an issue of power, money, control
the establishment of medicine as a profession
with university *training*
led men to bar women from the practice
long before *science* intervened.

they took command
over profits and prestige

while their patients perished
from unsterile surgeries
aggressive childbirth practices
faith-based medicines
pure arrogance.

## Europe 1300s to 1600s: Witches

a most egregious example.

men burned women healers at the stake
in Germany and England
both church and state
initiated, financed, executed
violent uncivilized practices
women stripped naked
    shaved
        tortured by thumbscrews
           the rack
                starvation
                    beatings.
accused of (gasp) female sexuality
    ravenous carnal lust
      membership in secret societies
        MAGICAL POWERS INFLUENCING
        HEALTH, HEALING, MIDWIFERY!

grasp of medical knowledge at the time:

Catholic Church: intercourse
deposits the homunculus (a teeny person with a soul)
who snuggles into the womb for a nine-month fattening up
only to be saved when baptized
by a (male) priest.

all sexual pleasure comes from the devil
all disease stems from sin, bad humors, and depraved temperaments
sin is God's punishment for evil.

*Genesis* takes on a whole new meaning.

     *In sorrow shalt thou bring forth children*
     *I will make your pains in childbearing very severe.*

common utterly ineffective *modern* (for the Middle Ages) medical
    treatments
      leeches

bloodletting
castor oil
(extremely toxic sometimes
lethal) mercury.
(it took a sturdy body just to survive the therapy not to mention the
illness)

men have always wanted
to be on top (in every way)
women (by definition) dance with the devil
dirty
contaminated by menses
shamed
fertile
dangerous by nature.

witch-like.

## 1600s to 1800s: Early America—Doctors Take Over Midwifery

in the colonies
on slave plantations
where life was short and babies plentiful
midwives were busy, respected, successful.

pregnant women, mostly young, healthy, prolific
labored, birthed, recovered
often in special borning rooms
pushed their babies out perched on birthing stools
surrounded by female attendants and family
a touch of folk medicine, tincture of opium, medicinal teas
magnetic lodestones, belladonna.

outcomes were usually good.

in the 1750s
men returned from prestigious European medical educations
midwifery was their first professional work
demand was high.

in Paris, they studied the process of birth
on poor women
measuring the size of the pelvis
manipulating the fetal position
espousing the idea that midwifery was a science
not magic or punishment from a wrathful God

      but they rarely washed their hands.

in England uneducated barber-surgeons developed
brutal methods to kill, slice, and crush the fetus
to save the life of the mother
which seldom turned out well.

      and they rarely washed their hands.

in the early 1600s, Peter Chamberlain invented two cupped spoons
to be slid over the fetal head
drag the baby out without destroying it.

he called his invention: forceps
kept it a family secret for more than one hundred years
operating under a sheet in the dark
so no one could see
guarding his trademark
and his profits.

French science, increased understanding of anatomy
English forceps got together (the secret was out)
to promote the superiority of male midwifery
extolling dangerous mid- and high-forceps deliveries
which spread to the American colonies.

after 1800 man midwives drove lady midwives out
by shortening labor using forceps
except (of course) when it came to the poor.
(no profit there)

and they rarely washed their hands.

## 1800s: Ignorance Meets Modesty

male midwifery
was the only part of medicine
dosed with a modicum of science.

for educated docs
a middle and upper class gentlemen's profession
diplomas and apprenticeships only for men
of appropriate social class
elite MDs trained in places like Harvard
the poorly educated in proprietary profit-making schools.

they all had no (I repeat NO) practical knowledge.

that came after graduation.

it was soon considered unwomanly for a female
to be educated and attend births.

(how quickly they forget)

women were too weak and emotional
mentally crippled by menses
unsexed by medical school
unable to simultaneously be wife and mother.

male doctors needed to build their reputations
births were usually successful
doctors (not mothers) got full credit.

they renamed their specialty: obstetrics (Greek: to stand before)
competing sects emerged
        botanists
                homeopaths
                        hydrotherapists.

patients expected doctors to DO SOMETHING!

doctors felt a need to DO SOMETHING!
        more ice
                more emetics
                        more mustard plasters.

common beliefs flourished as truth.

> Dr. Charles Meigs 1792–1896 (father of ob-gyn)
> *[Woman] has a head almost too small for intellect and just big enough for love.*
> middle and upper class women experience more difficult deliveries
> than sturdy farm women
> female education produces a small pelvis and a baby with a large head
> the poor and unmarried should not be cared for next to respectable women
> diseases and treatments vary according to social class
> illness is caused by miasma (bad air)
> inherited weaknesses, derelict lifestyles.

Victorian women experienced intense shame
over their bodies and ailments
birth became a public event
that challenged purity and privacy.
> (and implied sexual activity)

modesty was key, language danced around the messy physicality
> *pregnancy*: in a family way, expecting, in a delicate condition
> *confinement*: pregnancy and the postpartum state should be concealed
> > a time for women to withdraw from society
> *gyn disorders* reflected female misbehavior
> *birth* became a rite of passage: a moral and physical test judged by the male doctor.

there was actually a debate within the medical profession
should a doctor actually LOOK at the female body???
OMG, this could be a threat
to the *sanctity of female modesty and chastity*
> (Professor Meigs)
mostly, he worried about the doc's reputation
the accusation of being an *unchaste man*
clinical instruction was *grossly offensive alike to morality and common decency.*

when docs started practicing on poorhouse women
protest erupted, not in defense of the women
but on how this reflected on the respectability of the men.

doctors argued that they should practice by touch alone
and they did
averting their eyes, their hands groping
beneath layers of skirts and petticoats
research on hospital deliveries could ruin
a hospital's reputation.

a popular health movement blossomed
encouraging women
to get to know their own bodies
to demand control.

but doctors dominated the rules of social place
midwives gradually disappeared
for all but the poor and women of color
maleness meant safety
femaleness meant needing a man to take charge.

> meanwhile the men did not
> wash their hands.

they went from autopsies to women's bedsides to homes
nurses, ancillary staff, (from the Latin *ancilla* maid servant)
did not change their own bloodstained dresses or the patient's
  sheets.

childbed fever exploded and killed
hundreds of thousands.

> and no one washed their hands.

## 1700s to 1900s: Germs

the discovery that women bearing children were sickened and
      dying
from contagion
some ill humor passed from dead corpse to birthing woman
a doctor's hands and frock crusted in blood and pus
(a mark of experience and skill)
unwashed forceps
sickening the next laboring patient.

revolutionized medicine.

but it took a while, many decades
Dr. Meigs noted in the1840s

> *Doctors are gentlemen, and gentlemen's hands are clean.*

given that kind of arrogance, denial, and social hierarchy
it is not surprising that
the (relatively) good men when it comes to
the theory of contagion were also good scientists
ridiculed, outcasted, ignored
sometimes driven to lunacy.

> 1795 Alexander Gordon: disease is transmitted by birth
> attendants from one woman to another.
> (shocking)

> 1829 Robert Collins: childbed fever is due to unsanitary
> practices. He closed his hospital, cleaned and scoured
> everything, segregated the sick from the well, eliminated
> death from childbed fever.
> (ignored)

> 1842 Thomas Watson: birth attendants should wash their
> hands in chlorine solution and change their clothes
> between patients to avoid *becoming a vehicle of contagion
> and death between one patient and another.*
> (preposterous)

1843 Oliver Wendell Holmes: childbed fever is infectious, carried from patient to patient by docs and nurses. Advised clean clothes and body, avoiding autopsies on women who died of childbed fever. A physician with lots of cases of childbed fever and death is not a misfortune but a criminal.

(ridiculous, we're gentlemen, let's not worry the ladies)

1855 Ignaz Semmelweis demonstrated the contagion through observation and statistics. Required all attendants to wash their hands in antiseptic chloride solution before work and before each vaginal exam.

(scorned, humiliated, nervous breakdown)

1860 Louis Pasteur: diseases are caused by germs and can be prevented if germs are killed or stopped prior to infection. In 1880 he showed that postpartum women were susceptible to the bacteria, streptococcus.

(radical, ultimately celebrated)

1860s Joseph Lister: developed the concept of antiseptic surgery, disinfecting surgical instruments, surgical sites, wearing clean gloves, hand washing before and after surgery. (finally) He advised washing the postpartum genitalia four times a day with carbolic acid, but docs hands and syringes for douching were not disinfected, so childbed fever spread.

(mocked but ultimately accepted)

1930s along with the invention of penicillin and sulfa, childbed fever was conquered at last.

what took you so long?
you should have listened to the midwives who at least

didn't meddle.

oh right.

Doctor Knows Best!

## early 1900s: The Prep

okay let's do a reality check here
hospitals started as urban asylums for the poor, homeless, working
    class
rich ladies took to their plumped pillows and clean sheets
confined at home
a midwife or doctor
in attendance.

but as we reached the 1900s
women came to the hospital for safety
        pain relief during labor
              recuperation afterwards
what they got was more interventions
        more disease
            more death
                more students training on them
                    more male doctors trying
                        to control the whole
                          damn process.

in the never ending fight against contagion.

the good news:
        wards were aired and washed with carbolic acid
        nurses bathed and changed their uniforms.

the bad news:
        care of the pregnant woman at the illustrious University of
        Pennsylvania
        clean or shave pubic hair to remove dirt and lice
        remove woman's clothing
        give enema (poop was clearly a germ-filled embarrassing
            ickiness that got in the way of the doc's sterile field)
        start daily quinine (note: a malaria drug widely used in
            pregnancy into the early 1900s causing serious side effects)
        start drugs for constipation, headache, insomnia
        at onset of labor, give cathartic (which produces cramping
            and extreme diarrhea)

rupture amniotic membranes

apply forceps to baby's head

give shot of ergot after delivery of the head (ergot—a fungus
    that contracted the uterus, could cause uterine rupture,
    not to be used if high blood pressure, but who's
    checking that?)

after the birth, apply abdominal pressure to accelerate the
    delivery of the placenta

bathe woman right after delivery.

care of the pregnant woman at the prestigious Sloane
    Maternity Hospital

New York City

on admission: enema

followed by vaginal douche with bichloride of mercury

wash hair with kerosene, ether, and ammonia

wash nipples and belly button with ether (ouch)

shave pubic hair if charity patient
        (who are obviously dirty because they are poor
        or poor because they are dirty)

enema every twelve hours (ick avoidance again)

vaginal douche during and after labor with saline and
    whiskey or bichloride of mercury.

needless to say

these approaches didn't keep women safe.

they did routinize and dehumanize childbirth

the aggressive cleaning produced

more virulent bacteria

    more fever

        more pus

            more blood poisoning

                more funerals

                    more limp lifeless babies.

## 1813 to 1883: James Marion Sims

another big bad father of modern gynecology.

invented the vaginal speculum
      his attitude towards the distasteful task
      of treating women changed
      when he was faced with an enslaved woman
      who had fallen off a horse
      injured herself *down there*
      positioned her on all fours
      leaning forward
      shoved his fingers in to have a look
      he was inspired.

      later, bending the handle of a pewter spoon
      arranging mirrors
      for a better view.

      voilà, a speculum.

he figured out how to repair vesico-vaginal fistulas
      tears between the bladder and vagina
recto-vaginal fistulas
      tears between the rectum and vagina
(a good thing to fix).

occurred during prolonged difficult labors
causing the damaged mother
anguish, embarrassment
uncontrolled leakage of
      urine
          feces
              flatulence.

women smelled funky
took to their beds, devastated, outcasted
no longer attractive or useful
ashamed.

for his work, in 1876
Dr. Sims was named president of the American Medical Association
1880, president of the American Gynecological Society.

statues were erected
> a respectable-looking man with a high forehead
> patrician nose
> thick sweep of hair
> touch of jowl
> elegant bowtie
> clean conscience.

gracing New York City's Central Park
the statehouse in South Carolina
Philadelphia's Jefferson University, his alma mater
extolled nationally
decorated in Belgium, France, Italy, Spain, Portugal.

you should also know

Dr. Sims was an ambitious southern slave holder
Dr. Sims thought Black people did not feel pain like white people
Dr. Sims thought Black people were not as smart as white people
because their skulls grew too quickly
Dr. Sims operated on Black babies, using a shoemaker's tool
to pry their bones apart to loosen their skulls
100 percent fatal.

Dr. Sims conducted surgical experiments
on enslaved Black women WITHOUT ANESTHESIA
1841 to 1845 operating multiple times on each woman.

ether was available for pain relief
one year after he began his experiments.

the excruciating agony, screaming, fear, trauma
the naked woman on her knees, bent forward
while clusters of white men
peered up her vagina
observing the great man in action.

think about that.

the slave owners gave consent
they had a financial interest
in their property recovering
working, bearing children
they provided clothing, paid taxes
Dr. Sims took over temporary ownership
(or purchased if needed)
fed them
until treatment was completed.

for him, it was a perfect arrangement
he was happy.

when he wore his assistants out
other slaves held their fellow slaves down
while the doctor cut
       poked
             prodded
                    sutured
                            experimented.

Lucy, 18 years old
a baby a few months earlier
leaked urine ever since
surgery lasted an hour
perched on her knees, bent forward onto her elbows
her head rested in her hands
twelve doctors observing.

even Dr. Sims noted
*Lucy's agony was extreme*
after surgery
he allowed her opium
she developed severe infection
blood poisoning.

Dr. Sims wrote:

*I thought she was going to die . . .*
*It took Lucy two or three months to recover entirely*
*from the effects of the operation.*

Anarcha, 17 years old
traumatic labor and delivery
thirty operations over four years
without anesthesia
finally Dr. Sims declared he had *perfected* the procedure.

tried it on Lucy and Betsey to be sure.

those are the ones whose names he recorded.

now he was ready for white women
with anesthesia, of course.

Dr. Sims believed that infant lockjaw (neonatal tetanus)
(probably from infection of the umbilical cord cut with dirty
     instruments)
was due to pressure on the brain
best treated with his skull cracking procedure.

*Whenever there are poverty, and filth, and laziness, or where the
     intellectual capacity is cramped, the moral and social feelings blunted,
     there it will be oftener found.*

*Wealth, a cultivated intellect, a refined mind, an affectionate heart, are
     comparatively exempt from the ravages of this unmercifully fatal
     malady.*

when babies died, he blamed

*the sloth and ignorance of their mothers and the Black midwives who
     attended them.*

certainly not himself.

in the 1850s Dr. Sims
moved to New York
opened the first Woman's Hospital
testing his controversial surgeries on poor white patients.

during the civil war he moved to Europe
toured hospitals, operated on women with fistulas.
(possibly promoted the secessionist cause)

Dr. Sims returned to the US
to practice on wealthy women.

he became known for removing both ovaries and clitoris
to treat insanity
        epilepsy
                hysteria
                        nervous disorders
                                improper sexual behavior
at the request of the women's husbands.

racism and sexism
two thick branches on the sturdy trunk of
white male supremacy.

                        in 2021, Anarcha, Lucy, and Betsey
            were memorialized in Montgomery, Alabama
                   the statue titled *Mothers of Gynecology.*

## mid-1800s to 2000s: Darwinism, Eugenics, Sterilization

the dawning of the twentieth century
the birth of modern scientific methods
    observation
        hypotheses
            experimentation
the pollution of good ideas by the prejudices of the time.

Charles Darwin, (1809 to 1882) meticulously observed
Galapagos tortoises
    mockingbirds
        finches
            orchids
questioned breeders on farms
lovers of pigeons
came to understand the processes of natural selection
the development of species
apes to humans
survival of the fittest
a victory of science over faith.

Francis Galton, inspired by his half-cousin Charles
argued that desirable human traits
(as defined by those in power)
were inherited
(unrelated to education, economic conditions)
he called this (racist pseudoscientific) idea *eugenics*.

eugenicists scurried about classifying the *degenerates* and *unfit*
    poor
        mentally ill
        blind
            deaf
                developmentally disabled
                promiscuous
                    homosexual *deviants*
                    criminals

immigrants
racial groups. (Blacks, Asians, Jews- not actually a race)

in the late 1800's, thirty-eight US states banned marriage
between different races
1924 twenty-nine states still had a ban on interracial marriage.

lasted for forty-three more years
until the Supreme Court, Loving v. Virginia.

eugenicists argued these folks weakened the (Aryan/Nordic) race
   *undesirables* should be segregated
     institutionalized
      sterilized
       (possibly murdered)
        1896 Connecticut: epileptics and *feeble-minded* were
         forbidden to marry.

ON THE OTHER HAND

*desirables* (intelligent, upper class, white)
were encouraged to procreate!
     PROCREATE!
# PROCREATE!

selectively mate to improve the human species
breed out the unwelcome, misbehaved, darker elements of society.

1903 President Theodore Roosevelt warned of *race suicide*: opposed
     birth control
      for middle and upper class
      white Anglo-Saxon Protestant women
1911 the Race Betterment Foundation established a pedigree registry
working class women were accused of
     biological warfare as *breeders*
back in jolly England, Winston Churchill supported eugenics
to solve *race deterioration*
reduce crime and poverty.

so what does this have to do with ob-gyn?

early twentieth century programs developed
to stop *undesirables*

from ruining everything
through forced sterilization.
(done by ob-gyns)

1907 Indiana, first compulsory sterilization laws
(overturned 1921)

1909 to 1979 California, more than 20,000 sterilizations
on people in state mental institutions

1927 US Supreme Court ruled Carrie Buck
a young woman institutionalized after being
raped and impregnated
could be forcibly sterilized
as Supreme Court Justice Oliver Wendall Holmes famously
quipped
*three generations of imbeciles are enough*

1930s Puerto Rico implemented a sterilization program for poor
women

thirty-three states allowed involuntary sterilization of anyone
deemed unworthy
the *promiscuous* (often destitute children of Mexican, Italian,
and Japanese immigrants)
sexual deviants
more likely if you had a Spanish surname
or were African American, poor, disabled, institutionalized.

in the south they called it
a *Mississippi appendectomy*.

legislators, social reformers, doctors advocated
sterilization as a public health intervention
to remove defective genes from society
decrease the social and economic costs of dealing with
*degenerate stock*.

the Nazis were inspired
by the US eugenics movement.

WE KNOW HOW THAT TURNED OUT.

by 1961, over 60,000 people had been sterilized
    based on eugenics
    the majority were women

1970 to 1976 up to 50% of Native Americans were sterilized
    consent unclear

1970s to 1980s Black women continued to be sterilized without
    knowledge or consent

2006 to 2010 California, 146 women received tubal ligations in
    prison
        majority first-time offenders
        African American or Latina
        many in violation of informed consent processes.

surgeons bragged they were saving the state money.
(no more welfare babies)

2017 Tennessee judge ordered a 30-day prison sentence reduction
        if incarcerated men and women agreed to be sterilized

2020 accusations of involuntary hysterectomies in
        US Immigration and Customs Enforcement facility.

every one of these operations involved
a doctor
willing
to do it.

## 1800s to 1900s: Birth of the Modern Obstetrician-Gynecologist

## pregnancy is divided into three trimesters.

### first trimester

[teeny clump of cells burrows into the uterus and starts the business of creating a home, 24-hour food service, the beginning of a tadpole existence and fluttering bubble of a heart]

in the before times
physicians
    asexual, Christian, paternalistic, respectable, ignorant
women (upper class women anyway)
        pious, pure, submissive, so delicate that leaving home while
        in a family way
        might produce severe nervous shocks damaging the
        reproductive organs.
        (oh no)

then
Science Happened
        germs wiggled under microscopes
        French chemist Louis Pasteur squinted at magnified globules
        of yeast, chains of bacteria
        doctors and nurses washed their hands
        Joseph Lister proselytized sterile surgical technique
        a quirky dentist, William Thomas Morton
        publicly gave a patient inhaled ether
        for a remarkably painless tooth extraction
        every surgeon wanted *that*.

        manufacturers cranked out sterile sutures, dressings, cotton,
            gauze
        metal surgical scissors, forceps, tweezers, scalpels
        could be ordered from an illustrated catalogue
        sterilized after each use

the first blood bank was established
affording life-giving transfusions for women
bleeding to near death during childbirth or miscarriage.

a critical addition to obstetrical care.

modernization was a bumpy ride.

1851 the American Medical Association advised
against the use of the speculum
too embarrassing for women
too dangerous for (asexual, Christian, paternalistic, respectable)
doctors' reputations.

it took a while.

another big female problem
(noted by Hippocrates four hundred years before the crucifixion)
PROLAPSE
            various pelvic organs and supports
                        weakened by repeated childbirth, heavy physical
                        labor, poor nutrition
                    fell out
                            *down*
                                    *there.*

(the evolutionary price for standing upright)

this very-smart-about-a-lot-of-things-but-not-everything, ancient
      Greek physician
recommended applying astringents to the sorry uterus
then stuffing it back into the vagina
with a sponge soaked in vinegar and half a pomegranate
to plug the whole thing up.

if that didn't work, there was always tying a woman upside down
bouncing her until her organs plopped back in
or by 1603, scaring the uterus into the vagina
by waving a red hot iron
in its vicinity.

by the 1700s, the stuffing-something-in-there technique won out
physicians settled on The Pessary

lint balls, halved fruit, brass, waxed cork, silver, gold
some with threads to pull them out
some connected to external wire cages to hold everything in.

(along with usual astringents, douches, inoculation with gonorrhea
    to produce infection and scarring, leeches . . .)

## second trimester

[fetus looks more like a little person with a big head at an acrobatic
swim meet working hard at getting all its organs on the road to
maturity]

1844 Charles Goodyear changed everything
US patent no. 3,633
the invention of vulcanized rubber
gynecologists seized the opportunity
an explosion of rubber pessaries of
various imaginative sizes and shapes
burst onto office shelves
contraptions, part plug, part doughnut
the doctor as expert with a product to sell
            insert
                    remove
                            clean
                                    reinsert.

good for business and a man's reputation
good for suffering women.

ladies paid attention
they wanted a male expert
painless labor
something that actually improved their ailments.

a healthy functioning reproductive system
being a measure of a woman's
personal and social worth.

conservatives pushed back
argued ether and chloroform during childbirth
    violated god's biblical curse on women
        argued birth pains were key to induce
        mother-love
            argued women were born to suffer.

upper class women in tight corsets synched to 15-inch waists
tended towards weakness, fainting spells, deformed rib cages and
    hips.
(they could barely take a deep breath, for Christ's sake)

some women were invalided
by vaginal and urinary tract infections, syphilis
intolerable odors, discomfort.

but a strange phenomenon happened on the way
to the birth of
the modern obstetrician.

by the 1920s, obs believed
*normal* births were so rare
interventions were required.

1923 a respected Boston ob remarked
    birth is not *something natural and normal*
    *and not worth the time and specialists' charges*
    but *a complicated and delicately adjusted process*
    *subject to variations from the normal*
    *which may be disastrous to the mother or baby or both.*

Dr. Joseph DeLee (a big daddy of ob)
declared two hours of pushing that baby out
    were the limit.
    (based on no data whatsoever)

he advocated routine
    sedation with ether in labor
    cutting the vagina (episiotomy)
    forceps to pull the baby out
    ergot to contract the uterus

extracting the placenta with pressure on the abdomen
stitching the perineum to *virginal conditions.*
        (dream on Joe)

he stated
(based on no data whatsoever)
        these practices prevent damage to the mother's pelvic floor
        brain damage to the fetus
        a life of crime for the kid.

        *Unaided birth is like a woman falling on a pitchfork*
        *a baby's head getting stuck in a door jam.*

Labor is pathologic: *So frequent are these bad effects, I have often*
        *wondered whether*
        *Nature did not deliberately intend women to be used up*
        *in the process of reproduction*
        *in a manner analogous to that of salmon*
        *which dies after spawning.*

and thus the rules were born.


### third trimester

[fetus rapidly puts on the pounds, homeland is getting crowded, the
kid gets ready to leave its underwater digs and has mastered thumb
sucking, opening its eyes, listening, squirming, peeing, and pooping]

modern women clamored for birth control
ventured outside (in a family way) in their new mail order
Lane Bryant maternity clothes
finding public nursing scandalous
tried bottle feeding
which turned out less fatal for babies
once sterilization was finally understood and adopted.

women were taking charge and fainting less.

feminists and suffragettes campaigned for twilight sleep
wealthy society ladies formed the Twilight Sleep Association

docs preferred passive medicated laboring women
who (hopefully) would come back for more
discover the joys of traditional femininity
save the Anglo-Saxon race from oblivion.

in rural and poor urban settings
states developed child hygiene bureaus
to prevent high infant mortality
they upgraded or outlawed
      untrained
            superstitious
                  sometimes unclean
                      midwives
attacks awash in racialized and ethnic slurs.

1933 a White House conference on child health
found NO decrease in maternal mortality
or increase in fetal survival
in the past 15 years
despite prenatal care
      hospital deliveries
            aseptic technique.

standards for prenatal and hospital care were lacking
excessive interventions occurred
birth injuries and unnecessary C-sections were way up.

regulations exploded
better training for docs and nurses
      blood banks
            oxytocin to stimulate contractions
                  x-ray pelvimetry to measure the pelvis in
            labor
                      spinal and epidural anesthesia
                        less mid and high forceps
                          IVs for everyone
                            routine fetal
                              monitoring.

1940s penicillin changed the threat of infection.

women delivered on their backs
legs splayed in stirrups
draped in sterile sheets as if for a major surgical procedure.

for decades
private docs opposed any federal legislation
to improve maternity care
to create national health insurance
blaming women's ignorance
or failure to seek care
as the cause for high rates of death and disease.

private insurance rarely paid for prenatal care
sick pay did not cover birth
          (for insurance companies birth was a natural process
          not a disease)
Medicaid (support for low income families) did not pass
          until 1965.

there were rumblings and protests
various attempts to make childbirth
a natural, less anxious, safer, more spiritual experience
a learned skill, an ecstatic athletic event
the fulfillment of a woman's life and destiny.

obs didn't like this trend
awake demanding empowered women
were time consuming
                              unruly
                    unnatural
                                        unpredict
                                                able.

epidurals almost put an end to that.

# birth

[confusing emergence into a dry, bright, noisy world full of
expectations, breathing being the first order of business]

on July 1, 1975, the first day of my residency
I took a deep breath
wandered anxiously into Boston's Beth Israel Hospital
exhausted from a weekend move from New York City
my internship over
immediately lost in the crisscrossing corridors
the hustle of staff in scrubs and white coats.

I walked into a conference room
past the doughnuts and coffee
sat quietly in the back
stared across the heads of an almost entirely older white male staff
the very esteemed professor and department chief
alone in the front row to the left.

no one dared sit too close.

this was the state of the field I had chosen
I wasn't sure I could
survive and flourish.

but I did.

my story more stepping stones and mudpuddles
hands stretched over ravines
women holding each other up
as we juggled too many flaming torches.

# Note

some of the names and dates have been changed
to protect the innocent
the guilty
and everyone in between.

but all events are essentially true to the best of my memory.

# Acknowledgments

This poetry came to me mostly in moments of quiet while hiking, biking, dreaming, searching through boxes of letters, collected bits of paper, photo albums, arriving in no particular order, one opening line leading to another cascade of memory, tugs of emotion, as the memoir was born and took shape. It was a strange, obsessive, exhilarating process that needed to be wrestled into a coherent story grounded in a historical context, researched, reworked, words honed and fussed over. While the writing was a deeply personal and solitary journey, I immersed myself in a diverse community of family, friends, colleagues, activists, poets, stakeholders, agents, to read the poems, offer advice, support, and correction. I am particularly indebted to my astute and enthusiastic critique group, "The Persisters," Lauren Clark, Michelle Griskey, Severine Patak, and Mary Sloat, for their sisterly feedback, laughter, perspectives, and belief that this work had meaning and value.

# About the Author

**Alice Rothchild** is a physician, author, and filmmaker who loves storytelling that pushes boundaries and engages in unexpected conversations. She practiced obstetrics and gynecology for almost 40 years and served as Assistant Professor of Obstetrics and Gynecology, Harvard Medical School. She received Boston Magazine's Best of Boston's Women Doctors Award, was named in *Feminists Who Changed America 1963–1975*, had her portrait painted for Robert Shetterly's Americans Who Tell the Truth project, and was named a Peace Pioneer by the American Jewish Peace Archive. Learn more about Alice at https://alicerothchild.com/